A Garland Series

The English Stage
Attack and Defense 1577 - 1730

A collection of 90 important works
reprinted in photo-facsimile in 50 volumes

edited by
Arthur Freeman
Boston University

Antitheatrical Tracts
1702-1704

with a preface
for the Garland Edition by

Arthur Freeman

Garland Publishing, Inc., New York & London

1974

Library of Congress Cataloging in Publication Data
Main entry under title:

Antitheatrical tracts, 1702-1704.

Reprint of A scourge for the play-houses, by
R. Burridge, first published 1702, London; of Stage-
plays arraigned and condemned, by W. Ames, first
printed 1702, by A. Baldwin, London; of An humble
application to the Queen, and her great council, the
Parliament of England, to suppress play-houses and
bear-baitings, with all prophaness and immorality, by
J. Feild ⌈i.e. Field⌉ first printed 1703, by T. Sowle,
London; and of A letter from several members of the
Society for Reformation of Manners, to the most reverend
father in God, Thomas, by divine providence, Lord Arch-
bishop of Canterbury ⌈Dec. 10, 1704⌉
    1. Theater--England--History--Sources. 2. Theater--
Moral and religious aspects.
PN2593.A5 1974   792'.0942   77-170480
ISBN 0-8240-0627-5

Contents

Preface

Four essentially noncontroversial attacks on the stage, not strictly attached to the Collier affair, are included in this volume. Richard Burridge's Scourge for the Play-Houses *(1702) is not in Sister Rose Anthony's checklist of "interim" writings, but is discussed by Hooker (I, 502); it is remarkable for its vehement objection to the sacrilege of representing heavenly phenomena like thunder and lightning in theaters, a practice returned to with renewed interest immediately after the great storm of 26-7 November 1703, in* A Representation of the Impiety & Immorality of the English Stage *and in Collier's (?)* Some Thoughts *concerning the* Stage *(both 1703). We reprint Burridge's* Scourge *from the Folger copy (PN 2047 B9), collating A-D⁴ (Lowe-Arnott-Robinson 342).*

William Ames's Stage-Plays Arraigned and Condemned *is an echo from the past, for the great self-exiled puritan scholar ("Amesius") died in 1633 in the damp air of Rotterdam. He is referred to here as "Professor of Divinity of Francker [i.e., Franeker] in Friesland," a post he occupied for over a decade. The influence of Ames upon American thought is well documented, commencing even before his widow and children sailed*

7

PREFACE

to New England with his large and valuable theological library, which may be justly called the first really significant accumulation of books established on North American soil. A remarkable collection of Ames and Amesian materials toward a full study of his works was assembled by the late Douglas Horton, and has since passed to the Andover-Harvard Theological Library. Stage-Plays Arraigned and Condemned *is scarcely representative of a neo-Calvinist revival, but is rather an arbitrary linking-up of a celebrated scholiast of the past with latter-day hostility to a far different stage from Ames's model. We reprint a copy at the Houghton Library, Harvard (*Thr 417.02.3), collating A-B² (Lowe-Arnott-Robinson 341).*

John Feild's Humble Application *to Queen Anne to suppress playhouses includes in its targets bear-baiting — a combination which would trouble the ghost of an earlier Queen, who went so far as to set aside a drama-free weekday for her favorite entertainment at the Bankside Gardens. Of Feild himself I know nothing; his petition is dated 10 December 1702, months only after Queen Anne's accession, and we reprint the British Museum copy (4152.f.23[25]), collating A-B⁴ (Lowe-Arnott-Robinson 343).*

The brief Letter *of 10 December 1704 to Archbishop Thomas Tenison ("that dull man," as James II called him) is specifically in protest of the appointment of Vanbrugh as manager of the new*

PREFACE

Haymarket theater. The old objections are tricked out again, with citations from his plays to prove his own irreverence and immorality. Vanbrugh did not answer. One wonders if the members of the Society for Reformation of Manners recalled that Tenison had preached the funeral sermon for Nell Gwynne. We reprint a copy at the University of Texas, collating [ ] ², with drop-title only (Lowe-Arnott-Robinson 344); this has been somewhat reduced for the sake of convenience.

May, 1973   A. F.

9

A

SCOURGE

FOR THE

Play - Houses :

OR. THE

CHARACTER

OF THE

English - Stage.

By *Richard Burridge.*

LONDON,

Printed for the Author, and are to be Sold by the
Booksellers of *London* and *Westminster.* 1702;

The Epistle

TO THE

READER.

Candid Reader,

*I*T *Being my Misfortune, to enjoy too
much the Pleasures of this World,
the Taste of which all Men Desire, I had
at length an utter Aversion to the Irregularities committed through the Delusions thereof : Whereupon,* (*as soon as I
had written the Satyrs, Intituled, Saint*
Ignatius's Ghost, The Shoemaker beyond his Last, Hell in an Uproar, *and*
The Apostate Prince, *design'd by me for
one Book,* (*but persuaded by the Bookseller*

for his Interest, to Print them single)
I was Paraphrasing Don Quevedo, *be-*
cause it sharply touched the Vices which
are so much in Fashion with the Liber-
tines of this present Age: having turn'd
the first Vision called the Algouazil, or
Catchpole, *into Verse, I was Intreated*
by a Gentleman, to let him shew the Co-
py to Sir Roger L'Estrange, *who ha-*
ving strictly perused it, return'd it by his
Amanuensis, *desiring (but without any*
Reason) it might not be Printed; accor-
dingly I burnt the Manuscript, at the same
time reflecting on him, as a Gentleman of
prodigious Parts and Learning, but as bad
a Poet as Cicero, *whom* Catullus *thus*
justly Censures :

Tanto pessimus omnium poeta,
Quanto tu optimus omnium patronus.

However, being inveterate against
the Immorality of the Times, I was Re-
solved to expose the Play-houses, *the very*
Common-

Common-shore of all *Filthiness*, by giving the *World* an impartial *Character* of it : But if it should touch any so much, as to bring from them a *Curse* for the *Author*, know *I* value as little thy *Censure*, as *I* have reason to *Envy* thy *Conversation*, and *I* dread as much thy *Applause*, as *I* scorn thy *Derision* ; if the *Phrase* in many *Places* is *Tart* and *Provoking*, *I* hope it will appear, that *I* *Study* not to *Please*, but *Lash* : *As* it is, now, my great *Charity* for every *Man*, to wish that part of him best, which he seems to regard least, *I* cannot but cross the *Humour* of my *Friend*, rather than flatter his *Vice* ; and if the *Judgment* of those who *Write* to the *Theatres*, or play the *Fool* in them, or haunt such *Houses*, is not quite impaired, by an endless *Succession* of most *Sottish Debaucheries*, *I* do not doubt, but a great many will here see themselves, as not to be found *One* *Day* *Weeping* in the *Gulf* of *Sorrow* and endless *Amazement*. *I* am sensible, *I* shall set many *Ranters* about

bout my House, for telling the Truth, but their Winching will only divert Melancholly, and make me Laugh as heartily at such Asses, as Crassus, Sirnam'd Agelastus, who never Laughed but once all his Life, and that was at an Ass too, seeing him Eat Thistles. To make no longer Preambulation, I shall conclude by way of a short Advertisement, to a certain Irish Bard, which is to Notifie, That if he durst pretend again to defend the School of Hell, he would use more Wit and Sense, than he did in his Answer to Mr. Collier's View of that wretched Place; by which Attempt he has made himself so much a May-game to all Men of Sense, that it is now become an Adage to say, when one Reflects on a Blockhead, he Writes like C - - - - e : or if any other durst to take up the Cudgels, they shall have Hockly 'ith' Hole Play, A Clean Stage, and no Favour.

Know, I am next to Noble Oldham Born,
To Lash the Vices of the Age; and Sworn,
Like him, to Torture Knaves, like him, Contemn
What Pulpits, nor the Stage dare not Condemn.

A

SCOURGE

FOR THE

Play-Houſes, &c.

COMING One Morning from an Old *Barriſter's* in *Lincolns-Inn,* One as well known by the Poer, for his Oppreſſion, as a never-ſatisfy'd Uſurer for his Extortion : I came by the *New Theatre,* where, under the Pentiſe, I ſaw ſeveral of *Batterton's* Slaves, getting their Cues, or Parts, in the Sun-ſhine, in whoſe Faces, both Male and Female, any one might hold a good ſtock of Impudence, without much Skill in *Phyſignomy* ; ſome of 'em Walked as if they had endured great Fatigues, in a long Campagne of Lechery, who, were they to be put to the Teſt, had no doubt ſeveral Scars about them, to teſtifie they had really been in the Wars of *Venus* ; being ſo Rotten with often Fluxing and Salivating, that (like the *Apples of Sodom*) touch them, and they would fall to pieces : They being full of Breeding, *Good Morrow* was bid to one another, as they came to Rehearſe, with as much Joy, as an Arraigned Perſon cryes, *God Bleſs the King and the Honourable Bench,* when the *Jury* brings in their Verdict, *Not Guilty :* Some of 'em were well Accoutred through *Tally-man's* Faith ; and others again, were as bad Cloathed, as a *Taffy,* that is hung up for a Show on ſweet St. *Davy's*-Day ; but yet all Sworded, tho' but the meer Scum and Chippings of the Raſcality of the People : Here and there (I obſerved) one would be throwing his Paws abroad, and caſting up his Eyes, to'ards a Place that has thrown a Bill of Excluſion, againſt all their odious Profeſſion, long ago, then in a Magniloquent Voice cry out, — *O ! ye Gods.* Here was likewiſe attending the Inferior Wretches of this ſcan-
dalous

dalous Place, such as *Wardrobe-keepers*, *Barbers*, *Door-keepers*, *Porters*, and others, who are as tendable about their Business, as a *Jack Ketch* is in stripping the Executed Dead; and come sneaking there as duely for their daily Bread, as our broken Officer do to my Lord *R----h*'s Office for their Half-Pay.

Being weary with looking on the Buffoonry of such Fellows (who are all but Rogues and Vagabonds by Statute, alias, as they stile themselves before they come to *Vivat Rex*, His Majesty' Servants) I was going homewards, but accidentally Meeting a Gentleman of my intimate Acquaintance, he laid his Obligation so strict upon me, as to bear him Company to a Fish-Dinner providing in *Drury-lane*, at a Tavern which puts out for a Sign the resemblance of a thing which People, that are superstitiously Affected, commonly Nail on the Threshold of the Door to keep out *Witches*; at length I condescended to my Friend' Request, and went along with him to the Place aforesaid, which I found such Fellows as those of the *Guard du Corps*, and Mechanicks, frequently Resorted: Being entred into a Room pretty well fill'd with Gentlemen and Ladies, to save my self the trouble of shewing a great deal of Haviours to them severally, I made one Complement of the best and last Edition serve 'em all, howsoever Dignified or Distinguished, and then sat down with them as lovingly to the Peck, as a Parcel of *Tarpollians* do round a Platter of *Burgeu*; but hearing a Couple of Gentlemen, who undertook to Carve for the rest of the Company, cry one to the other, Chine that *Salmon*, Splat that *Pike*, Splay that *Brew*, Side that *Haddock*, Culpon that *Trout*, Transen that *Eel*, Tranch that *Sturgeon*, Barb that *Lobster*, &c. I began to listen, like a *Sow* in *Beans*, if I could hear any high Wind stirring, for I verily thought they were going to raise the Devil; but however, being as Refractory to fill my Belly, as Pope *Julius* the Third, who would have his *Pork* (forbidden him by the Physician) *al despetto de Dio*, in despight of God; I sat to it till I could Eat no longer.

Dinner being over, the Glass went briskly round till Four a Clock, and then my Friend, and some others, desired my Company with them to see a *Play*; so, rather than show my self Rude in not granting what they affectionately seemed to Desire, I went with them: But going thro *Play-House-Yard*, (where the Females were Flocking along as thick as *Seamen*'s Wives,

...ives, for a Game at *High Gammer Cook*, to *Portsmouth*, when they hear of the Fleet Anchoring at *Spithead* or *St. Helens*.) the Saucy Impudent Slut or another would, in a manner, be forcing their *Oranges* on us, talking some of them so Impudently, that I could no otherwise suppose, but that they had been debauch'd in the Mother's Womb, and so came acute Whores into the World : Now taking our *Tickets* for the *Pit*, into which I no sooner enter'd, but I thought it was very properly called; for no Place could more represent the Pit of Hell than that, there being no Light but by Fire, and the Discourse of those who were in it all Sinful and Prophane : We were no sooner Seated in this Academy of Sin, and Nursery of Uncleanness ; where poor Wretches make themselves expert in those Arts, whereby they most gratify Satan, and, as it were, in many open Bravadoes, Challenge the Almighty into the open Field, and dare Him to do the worst He can, I could not but remark the various Humours of the Place into which I was got : Some Ranters, by their Diabolical Discourse, seem'd to esteem nothing so Dangerous as real Goodness, and to Proclaim open Hostility against whatever shall bring along with it that unwelcome Charity of Preserving them from Hell : Some Sparks, by their Manners, show'd it was Base and Ungenteel to Fear a God, to Own a Law, or Practice a Religion ; saying, That Man was a Clown, who was not Proud of being thought a Sinner, and would not, without all Scruple, Proclaim himself an Atheist : Other some again, who had shaked Hands with their Reason, would, tho God had made them Men, prove themselves to be their own God, by a Second Creation, in endeavouring, by their filthy Discourse, to make themselves Brutes : Others by their frequent Swearing, seemed to cry out upon *Eve* for a lazy and dull Sinner, whilst in every Oath they Swore, That Soul was not worth a Damning, which cannot Sin without a Temptation ; neither was any Discourse they had, less Filthy than Malicious against Vertue ; so Foul, Obscene, and Nauseous were their Words, that those who were as little acquainted with a God as themselves, might be apt to conclude, That Nature had spoil'd them in the making, by setting their Mouths at the wrong end of their Bodies : In Fine, most of them were trickt up in such Gauderies, as if they had resolved to make their Bodies a Lure for the Devil, and with this Bravery would make a Bait, that should Tempt the *Tempter* to fall in Love with them.

B

Looking

Looking upwards, I saw the Upper Galleries was taken ⟨w⟩ by such Rubbish as *Butlers, Chamber-Maids,* quacking *Apothec ries,* and *Apprentices,* who were sneakt out to give some Swee heart, that an Hundred to One might be a Kitchen-wench, Washer of *Gause, Exchange* Girl, or *Sempstress,* a *Play* ; me while their Masters are at Home, fretting and fuming for wa of 'em to look to their Shops, till they go to the *Coffee-hou* to talk of the taking of more Towns over a Dish of *Tea,* th an expert General is able to take in Twenty Years Service Among this Fry, Crowd in at the last Act, all the Skip-ke nels that are in Waiting, they claiming this Priviledge in Rig of their Masters being Benefactors to the *House of Pollution.*

In the middle *Gallery* sat the middling sort of People, su as Merchants Wives, and Shop-keepers Froes, who being hig Fed and Pamper'd, come there to be Gallanted ; among who creep Ladies Waiting-women, *Lawyers Clerks,* and *Valet de Cha bres,* as likewise some Inferior sort of Town-Misses, who, spr cing themselves with prickt up Ears of Joy, are in hopes of i snaring some unthinking *Woodcock* or another ; for all of the Trade are as dexterous at Lying, Wheadling and Cheatin as a Victualler is in drawing the Geometrical Figures of Line Circles, and Semicircles, without a pair of Compasses.

In the side Boxes (I saw) were got upstart Officers, young Brothers, who most an end Live by their Wits, and other pra matical Beaux, Complimenting and Courting a parcel of Strun pets, who, by their Debauchery, and running away with *Ho land* Sheets from their Lodgings, had made shift to purcha themselves *Velvet* Hoods and Scarfs ; having their Masks on, th Inamoratoes took them at a Venture ; for one of our Sparl was Wasting that little Rhetorick he had, upon a Jelliver th was so Old, (but only put off with Patch and Paint) that, by cour of Nature, she must shortly follow her Teeth, which had bee gone before her these Thirty Years and better ; but, as the sa ing is, *A T - - d is as good for a Sow as a Pancake,* so any thin goes down with such Nifeys, who have no more Guts in the Brains, than the People of that Barbarous Nation, that Co demned, Executed, and ript up an *Ass,* to recover the *Mo* out of his Belly, which they supposed he had Swallowed, be cause they saw him drink at the Water, where the *Moon* ap peared by Reflexion ; and immediately thereupon (she bein mus

uffled up with Clouds) they miffed her : But feveral come
re, who, though they have too much Senfe for a Juftice of
ace, yet have too little for a Wife Man.

In the front Boxes fat Perfons of Quality, fome legitimately
orn, and fome who might Pray for a Whore as long as they Live,
elfe they never had had the good Fortune to be what they are;
me of them were beftowing Complements on common Har-
ts, huff'd up with fo many Hyperbolical Expreffions of their
eauty, that they could not chufe but fufpect they only la-
our'd how to be Difbelieved, or had Learned of their Dogs
ow to Fawn and Flatter ; and the fad Truth is, fome of our
obility and Gentry who were there, are fo far from being
eligious, that they are afhamed of nothing fo much, as that
y Man fhould have the Charity to think them fo : As they
e Noblemen, they think it below them to be Beggars at the
ates of Heaven, and do as much fcorn to fay their Prayers,
beg their Bread ; they hold Devotion and Humility are
ames wholly inconfiftent with Bravery and Gallantry ; 'tis
r fuch Faint-hearted Creatures (they think) as have not the
ourage to undergo with Alacrity, the Torment of Hell-fire,
ftoop fo low, as to beg an Heaven on their Knees : But
hy talk I of Religion among Perfons of Quality, when Luxury
d Debauchery is the only Mode among them ? But if thofe
wo Vices fo much predominant now a-days, be the Marks
true Religion, then indeed I muft confefs, we have more
odly Gentry in *England* than I thought of.

I could have named in particular all the Fools that fat there,
t that it is dangerous meddling with Nobles. As for the
Vomen-kind, who likewife fat among them, I could not well
ftinguifh common Jilt from Jilt of Quality : But I faw they
ere all as well pleafed with the Diverfion of Sinning, as an
lderman is in Snorting at a Sermon ; like my Lady F---l,
ey Love their Pleafures better than their God.

Thought I to my Self, if this is the Place vvhere a Man
ay Learn Morality, as thofe who are fo complacently Ac-
ffary to their own Ruine, fo obftinately beat upon, and fo
llicitoufly Studious of their own Overthrow, do alledge, *Old-
ick* fhould go to Learn Manners in a *Play-Houfe* for me ;
here I obferved nothing paffed but diffembling Language, covert

Engage-

Engagements, and cunning Flatteries, between Whore and Cull
I am sure, since, in this Age, Mankind of himself is too a
to grow so stupid in their Sins, as to fall in Love with Hel
Infatuated even to a Confidence in those Vanities, which ar
worse than nothing, and besotted into a Sensuality below what
Brutish, the *Theatres* are the worst Places which Old or Youn
of either Sex, can frequent ; but seeing too too many are A
fected with such vain Pastimes, I shall trouble my self no othe
wise about them, than in bestowing the Blessing of Cardin
Caraffa upon such Sinners, who (when the People flocked t
him in great Multitudes to be Blest by him, at making h
Entrance into Paris, as *Legate* from the Pope) lifting up h
Eyes devoutly to Heaven, and making, according to their manne
Crosses, instead of the accustomed Form of Episcopal Benedict
ion, Blessed the Honest vulgar *Frenchmen* in these Words, *Quand
quidem iste populus vult decipi, decipiatur*, if so be this People wi
be Gull'd or Deceived, (he meant with such Shows or Fopp
ries) let them be Deceived.

But now to the Manners of the *Pit* again, where, to pa
away the Time till the Anticks began to show their Trick
some could find no better Discourse, than to be talking an
giving their Judgments of the Ladies, and Fashions of the Times
where was the best Wine ; finding faults with their *Taylor*
and commending another's ; at length I was got in a Woo
for I was gazing, with as much Admiration as our Countr
Bumpkins do on the *Monument*, or Tombs in *Westminster-Abbe*
on some who were making, as they talk'd, *Spanish* Shrugs, an
French Smirks and Faces ; and then pulling out their Watche
to show they had such Moveables, to help out at a Dead Lif
by allowing 30 per Cent, and more, to have them laid up i
Lavender.

Some Prodigal Coxcombs mimick'd their Tones as finely a
the *Ischnotes*, who (as you may see in *Lilly's* Grammar) sa
Nync for *Nunc*, *Tync* for *Tunc*, &c. and amidst all their Talk
ing, Hand and Foot do so point, accent, and adorn their Lard
ed Stories with Fantastick Flourishes, that their Words are a
often lost in their Actions, as their Sense in the Words :
observed the Perriwigs and Coats of these Fops were so muc
bedawb'd with *Powder*, that I took them for a Company c
Millers, going to some Wake to be Drunk ; but looking wistl
agai

again in their Faces, which were disfigur'd with *Rodigero's* Commodity, from nasty Nostrils to the very Ears, I then took 'em for a Race begot by that strange Creature which was brought from *Africa*, and shew'd at *Moncrief's* Coffe house, behind the Fabrick built by *Gresham*; for all the City-Cuckolds to Rendezvouz at every Day, from Twelve till Two.

One Whisk, who carry'd his Hat under his Arm, for fear of depressing his Hair Helmet, which hung down to his very Posteriors, I observed, made, to show his Postures, a very submissive Congee to a Tovvn-Miss, so very lovv, that I thought he vvas going to Kiss his Shadovv, taking as much Care in his several Motions, as a Gentleman-Usher does in Handing, Arming, Siding, Dravving out, Presenting, Shouldering and Footing his Lady ; Svvinging his Cane after a Foppish Manner, as an Action (he thought) very taking ; the Svvord vvas hung belovv his Reach, as a Signal he vvore it more for Foppishness than Use, vvhen a Just and Honourable Cause required it ; his Handkerchief, vvhich might be the Spoil of some Female Combat, hanging half out of his Pocket ; and his Hatband vvora on the Top of the Crovvn, to decipher he vvas Maggot-pated ; being, after a great deal of Ceremony, sat dovvn, every novv and then he vvas looking on his Feet, because (as I suppose) his Shoes being rubb'd vvith *German*-Balls, serv'd his Fiz for a Looking-glass ; next one of his Gloves is pull'd off to admire his Hand, vvhich vvas not so Handsome nor so White, but only I imagine he vvas studying *Chiromancy*, and therefore vvas pondering on the Significancy of the Marks of his Bavvdy Fist : In a Word, he had as much Prodigality in him, as a Footman, vvho stands in a Morning at the Street-door, vvith one of his Master's *Diaper* Napkins on his Joulterhead, for a Night-Cap.

Some others were buzzing up in a Corner Words of a newer Coin than what Fools so much admire in *Butler's Hudibrass* ; which sounded as harsh in my Ears, as Words of that Language they Read at the *Jews* Synagogue, as Witches say their Prayers, backwards.

I saw here some Self-conceited Ninny-hammers, who were much of the Temper of *Fuller*, that indefatigable Spy of State, *i. e.* would be thought Gentlemen because ty'd to a Sword, not for Estate or Learning, on which last Account, the common Courtesie of *England* allows a Man that Title.

Here

Here Folks come (as Ladies do to Church) to see and be seen, and afterwards to the Tavern, to show what Proficient they are in the School of *Bacchus*, where they guzzle as stoutly as if they meant to carry. Liquor enough with them in their Bellies, to quench the Flames of Hell, or rather, as if they meant to drink themselves so far into Beasts, as they might thereby become incapable of Damnation: These I talk of now you must know, were Heroick Bullies, who are such Blades which make their Vices their Trade, trafficking first for a Living, and then for the State of *Dives*.

In another Nook sat a Flock of such Self-conceited Buzzards who have no better thoughts of Vertue, than to think their fine Cloaths may gain them a Respect, where *that* could not, and are Ambitious of thrusting themselves into all Companies, be they ever so Scandalous, if they have but fine Rigging, and a piece of Cold Iron dangling at their Asses, herein deviating much from a Gentleman indeed, who prefers the Wise Man in Rags, before the Fool in Robes; These were Complementing *Orange*-Wenches, who allow so much per Night, for the Priviledge of selling that for a Shilling in the House, which cost not Twopence, besides the Benefit of letting out their C————dities in Fee-tail after Play is over; in contracting which Bargain, they commonly Intail on their Purchasers aching Heads, gleating Yards, ulcer'd Bladders, sinking Noses, rotten Shins, and falling Palates, besides making some, under a severe Flux, surrender up their last Breath, in cursing the critical Minute, wherein they first laid Hand upon a Lady's *Merry-thought*.

Some again here, thought themselves (I warrant you) as brave Fellows as *Don Quixot*, when he fought the *Windmill*; at least Men of extraordinary Parts, because they could Talk High, Breathe Slashes, Thunder out big Words, and had stor'd themselves with so many insipid Jests, and Bombast, as tickled Asses, and stupified Fools: Some of our Acolasticks were got on the Stage, though 'tis desired to the contrary in their Bills, which are often stuft up with these Shams, *Acted by Command*; *at the Request of several Persons of Quality*, &c. There their Blockhead-ships were supporting the side Boxes, casting their Ogles about like handsome F——lding, to see if the Ladies took any Notice of their Apish Actions: Then, to shew their Shapes, they would walk to the other side in as great State, as the Water-
Bailiff

Bailiff with his Silver Oar, before a Gang of Pirates that are making their laſt Voyage to *Execution-Dock* ; and are as Offi-cious in flying at every Courtezan's beck, as a Beadle in run-ning round his Liberty, to give Notice to thoſe Bawds who ſee him, of a Private Search to be at Night:

Now I deſire all who are not Byaſs'd with the Intereſt or Love of Vanity, to tell me what Moral Precepts any can Learn of ſuch, whom I can compare to nothing but curious Guilt Volumes, ſtuft full of Erratas, and whoſe Heterogenious Souls are ſuch, that no leſs than a Combination of all the Vices in the World, muſt be Summoned in, to make up a partial De-ſcription of 'em ? Inſtead of going there to Reform, they go down-right to be Damned.

I obſerved Old Men here (the Wrinkles of whoſe Primitive Faces look'd as crabbed as the frightful Characters of the *Arabick* Alphabet) would ſplit their Ruby Caves at Viciouſneſs, and pick up Women, whom, by their Looks, compoſed of ſo much Sanctity and Innocency, as if they were going to ſuffer Martyr-dom, I could almoſt have ſworn had been as Chaſte as *Veſta's* Virgins ; but I found I was as much miſtaken in my good Opi-nion, as Mr. R———nd in *Cannon-ſtreet* was of his Daughter, whom he thought a Saint, but at laſt found to be a Devil Incarnate.

Sometimes the Fops would be attentively liſtening to the Mag-gots which *Purcel's* Train play'd on ſeveral ſorts of Inſtruments ; whoſe Miſchievous Harmony inſpiring the Auditors with Luſt, and Imaginations of Viſionary Joys, raiſed ſuch Optious Deſires in their roving Thoughts, as made them Mad to run over all the Women in the Houſe : To ſo high a Pitch is Debauchery Arrived there, that (like the *Sodomitiſh* Leachers, who would have Raviſhed Angels) they could ſcarce deſiſt from acting their Beaſtialities before one another's Faces. The Women (I took Notice) being ſmitten with the vairiety of Love-Tunes, by their wiſhful Glances, and leering from behind their Fans, had an Ebuli-tion in their heaving Breaſts, which ſignified their longing (like Grandam *Eve*) for Forbidden Fruit.

But at laſt, the Fellow that play'd at Bo-peep behind the Curtain, having made Report to the Patentees, there were Fools enough to bear the Charges of the Houſe, beſides a Pre-ſent

fent to them for their good Wills, in letting the Audience a
be Damn'd by Wholefale, it is drawn up, and the gawdy Scenes
are expofed to open View; then came ftrutting out, like a *Crow*
in a Gutter, one of thofe Fellows, whofe conftant Profeſſion
is an open Defiance to his Happinefs; who no fooner told hi
Canterbury-tale, but out came feveral, from feveral Appartment
of the Stage, clad in the Devil's Livery, upon whom I no
fooner caft my Eyes, but I faw too little to Love, enough to
Pity, more to Abhor, and in all too much to be Expreſs'd:
But, dear me! if there was clapping any Actor, he was Proud
of it, and as well pleas'd that he had Sinn'd with Applaufe,
as if they had tickled his A—ie with a Straw. I pity'd him for
his Folly, and fo do I all filken Beggars, who make themfelves
fuch miferable Wretches, as to trapan their own Souls out of
a Glorious Inheritance, for a Sorry Livelihood in this World;
making it their Maxim, if they fhould be Honeft, they are fure
to Live Miferable. Thefe fweet Babes of Grace had no fooner
play'd their Fools Parts, but in came fome more, whofe Character is fo bad, that I am not able to delineate it, unlefs I
compofe it of Wonder and Shame. Next came out a She piece
of ordinary Clay, ftuck round with *Briſtol* Stone, who Sinn'd
as Ingenioufly as the experteft of 'em: Now and then, I obferved a Beau would peep from behind the Shutters of Hell,
who is there admiring fome painted Sepulchre of an Actorefs's
Soul, Dead and Rotten in Trefpaffes and Sins; and at length,
by the help of *Satan*, (who is daily troubled with his Impor-
tunities of inventing variety of Objects, anfwerable to that
of his Humour) the lump of his Sin-fick Soul is Interred
with hers.

The Firft Act being ended, by that time the Serapers had
play'd a brisk Tune to the poor Fellow that Snuffs the Can-
dles, a Second begun: Then out came a Fool ftuft with Pro-
phanenefs, gliftering fo much with Tinfel and Spangles, that
he feem'd a Paradice full of Weeds, or an Heaven cramm'd
with Devils: After him were following Three or Four Pro-
methean Men or lumps of animated Dirt kneaded into humane
Shape, who if they have any fuch thing as a Soul, (which they
fhall hardly be able to perfuade any Man to believe, that fees
how little care they take to fave them) it is patched up with
as many Vices, as are Patches in a poor *Spaniard*'s Cloak:
Thus, whilft the Five Acts held, came out other Fools, in fuch

a

a fwaggering Pofture, as if they would feem to outbrave Damnation, and not be daunted with the thoughts of a future State, thinking a Retreat into Sobriety, would betray fuch an Effeminacy of Spirit, that might argue them in Love with a Religion, and make the World believe they were fuch Cowards as might be frighted into Piety. Between whiles a Song is Sung, by fome fuch Mifcreant, than whom no Man puts his Brain to more ufe ; for his Life is a daily Invention, and each Meal a new Stratagem : Likewife, before the Show is over, you fhall have fome great Dance, (who is commonly an Out-landifh Prig, of whom the Houfes make a noife of in their Bills, a dumb fign they want Cuftomers) fhowing his Activity, taking in his Dancing as much Care and Pains to new Mold his Body, as if the only Shame he fear'd, was the retaining of that Form which God and Nature gave him : Or, perhaps you fhall have a Jig performed by fome impudent Creature, who (though fhe is Five or Six Years in the Teens, and the Mother of a Baftard or Two) muft be called Mifs forfooth, which Childifh Name, it is to be feared, that having been fo long Mifapplied, it will at laft find the like hard Meafure, with thofe once more honeft Names of *Tyrant* and *Sophifter*, and from a Title of Honour, degenerate into a Term of the greateft Difgrace and Infamy ; it is indeed already made to be of no better a Signification than this, to denote a Woman of a Licentious and Lewd Life : Thefe Dancing Miffes (I minded) puffing out their Petticoats with quick twirling about, and making enticing Geftures with Hand and Foot, fet our Luftful Gallants Mouths a Watering, as bad as if they had been fucking *Lemons* : O the Curfe that hangs over this Nation ! For,

The Art of Leach'ry to that height is brought,
That daily all the Town's Debauch'd in Thought ;
From Nine to Ninety fhew the He or She,
That is in Mind or Fact from Whoring free ;
Were Thoughts but to be Clapt as well as Deeds,
The Lock *muft reach from* Southwark *to* St. Eads
Great Pox *in Triumph would ride thro' the Land,*
And with Infectious Scars the People Brand.
As ever Luft fo much in Man fhould Reign !
To make him feek for Ruine, Grief and Pain :
What Fools are we, to fpend our pureft Blood !
For that which doth our Healths more hurt than good:

C

The

The Pleasure that we Woo so to Enjoy,
As soon as Tasted, doth the Longing Cloy :
The greatest Beauty Poyson we may call,
And Woman Curse, for making us to Fall :
Ah ! if without Offence, it might be said
To Heaven, Nature should at first have made
Mankind, Deucalion *like, to propagate,*
Then had we 'scap'd our miserable Fate :
But whilst our doating Sex to them doth cleave,
Lost Paradice *we never shall retrieve.*

Now, to set out such who belong to any *Play-house,* I must needs say, the whole course of their Lives is a flat Contradiction to their Duty ; their constant Study is to teach their Bodies how to put Affronts upon their Souls, and to give him the Lye that dare tell them there are any hopes they may be Saved ; they Laugh at those who tell them there is any other Heaven than that of their own Creating, or any other Happiness besides their Pleasures ; if they have not leave to take every Day their full Carrier in Wickedness, they think their Souls bereav'd of their *Christian Liberty,* as if poor drowsy Sinners, they had no other way left them of imitating their Blessed Saviour, but by often descending into Hell : Poor Wretches ! their senseless Carcasses (for they have nothing in their Numb-Sculls, but what lewd Poets put in them) only cumber the Earth, and stink in the Nostrils of all good Men, as well as in the Nostrils of the Most High. They daily set themselves in Array against their own Happiness ; for they never think Death, Heaven's Disfigurer of Mankind, will Mark them, but always perfectly loathe and reject any thing that's Grave and Serious, as that which cannot suit with their rude Manners, and hellish Calling : Was I to take Notice how many Riots this Spawn of the Devil daily Commits, all those Frolicks and Revellings they are not only Guilty of, but Glory in, I should certainly lose my self in Admiration of their Madness : They are desperately Mad, with the fear of being counted Holy, and so ravenously Greedy of Eternal Destruction, that they would ever be tippling by their good Wills ; but as doubtless the Devil has Power over these Wretches when they are Sober, they need not give him the advantage of finding them so often Drunk, except in a Bravado they desire to show the World, how boldly they dare defie Heaven, and how much they scorn to owe their Damnation to any but themselves : When these Sots (who scorn to be over-ruled by any Body but strong Drink) are got together, with how much Complacency they draw up an Inventory, and Catalogue of all their sinful Extravagancies in Folio ; and when they fall to Drinking of Healths, not to admit of every one, it is no less than the greatest Disrespect and Injury that can be offer'd to the Person in Remembrance ; whosoever refuseth it, especially if it be a Whore remembred, they shall be sure to hear of it with an Oath now, and perhaps a Challenge anon : It is their Morning, Noon, and Evening-devotion, if they have Money or Credit, (which is but bad with the best of 'em, who Live but from Hand to Mouth all their Life-time) to be at a Drunken Revel, at which more Ceremony is used, and more Reverence by half to set it off, than to Grace the Worship and Service of God : All must be bare, and all upon their Knees, whilst a Catch is Sung instead of an Hymn : As for their talk, they take care how to vitiate their own Discourse, or the Minds of their Auditors, their subject being only the Mother of that thing which has the monstrous Shape of Sin : They bathe themselves in the filthy Puddle of Obscenity, suffering their talk to flag into an idle, and much more wanton strain of Drollery : I cannot but hear, with as much Wonder and Astonishment, as Pity and Compassion, those miserable Souls, which cannot invent no other Method of graceing their Discourse, and make it taking, but by talking of all Uncleannesses ; nor can they find Matter for an Hours Talk, without being beholden to an *Harlot* for it : They are so much Foes with God, that they suffer his Name to be so Vile and Cheap, as to be used only as an Expletive Particle to prevent a Chasm, or make up a Gap in the Sentence, or to make all run more Smoothly : In Fine, none of their Words are the Grave, Weighty, and well proportion'd Breathing of a great and pious Soul, but altogether the empty Bubblings of a restless Fancy, raging Lust, and frolicksome Humour, by which they shew themselves Poppits, not Men ; and only aim to be recorded hereafter, for inimitable Villanies : These poor Wretches of Actors, one part of the Year, when no Acting is, are forced to sharp and spunge about for Subsistance, lying daily obnoxious to such a Cheat, as to part with their own Souls in exchange for Vice : If at any time they finger a little Money, (which is but very seldom God wot) they make it the Opportunity of displaying their Vanities ; it is so habitual with

them

them to be Bad, that they take as much Pride to expose their Wickedness, as a Fool does to tell the Town, on *Valentine's*-day, what Trollip he has been Smuggling, by wearing her Name twisted round his Hatband ; and are as fond of seeing the Devil, as a young Maid her Sweet-heart on St. *Agnes*'s Night ; for whose Reception, the foolish Creature Washes her self stark Naked, and puts on a clean Smock : But however, seeing these Histrionian Reprobates will not go to Heaven with Spurring, St. *John*'s Curse, which he bestowed upon spiritual *Babylon*, be theirs, *If they will be Filthy, let them be Filthy still* ; and as their House has been burnt once already, so (provided no Houses else were hurt with it) it would be a Mercy, rather than a Judgment, if God vouchsafe to smite them once again.

But, whilst the *Play* was Acting, there were running in and out several of *Ovid*'s Heirs, who had all his Lasciviousness (tho' none of his Wit) entailed on them ; being most of 'em stockt as little with it, as that dubb'd *Physician*, who Writ a Satyr against it : In the *Pit* (for you must know the Rhyming Sparks have the Priviledge to go in when they please for nothing) I saw *Ravenscroft*, an old Standard to this House, a Man (I must needs say) who is endued with as much Sense, as the Fellow who went to find out *Time*'s Lodgings, to buy his Wings to make a Feather-bed ; and indeed, he Lives as handsomely now as ever he did in his Life, for in shifting his Creditors off so often, he has learnt to shift in the World. There was *Crown*, one that understands the *Ausonian* Language, just as that Pope who spoke false *Latin*, saying, *Fiatur*, for *Fiat in contemptum omnium Gramaticorum* ; yet I'll say that for him, tho' he knows nothing, yet he would not have the World know so much. Before the first Act was ended, starving *S.--le*, Poet Laureat to *Bartholmew* Fair, came blundering in, a long-known Sinner, and as old a Mumper, who sneaks into some Hall among the Whifflers every *Lord-Mayor's-Day*, for a Dinner ; he was ty'd to a Sword to, which lookt as comically on him, as to see an *Ale-draper*'s Wife in a Nightrail and *Muslin* Apron, to receive the droppings of the Tap, From behind the Scenes was peeping *M----x*, the *French* Bard, one that is an extraordinary Man in ordinary things, and is as well accomplished as *Pittis*, to Write Ballads for *Moor*, which Natural Parts make him as much in Admiration of himself, as the simple Fellow was of the Feather which dropped out of the Angel *Gabriel*'s Wing. There

was

was that *Hyternian* Poetaster *F----r*, one only (like the rest
of his Countrymen) a Wit in Jest, and Fool in Earnest; yet
by the Inspiration of *Usquebaugh*, has made shift to scribble
Two or Three *Plays*, one of which have had the Fortune to
take among Women, competent Judges I'll warrant you in such
Cases : But you must know, his Weak Brain has as hard a
Labour to bring any thing into the World, as the Countess
of *Zeeland* had, when she was brought to Bed of an *Almanack* :
And there was that old Tipple-pitcher *D----fy*, such a true
Bacchanalian Priest, that he holds there is no such Sanity, as
to be Sick with the *Staggers*, and the sweetest Life is to be
Dead Drunk : His Parts are much like the Man's last mentioned,
being as much plagu'd to bring any thing to Perfection, as *Mer-
cury* was in cutting out a Suit of Cloaths for the *Moon*, by
reason she was never of one bigness : I take him to be some-
thing of a Botcher as well as a Songster, by his patching up an
old Song that was made against the *Roundheads*, in the time of
the last Civil War, to deride an Ingenious Gentleman, that
Writ against the Immorality and Prophaneness of the Stage ;
in Answer to which, I have made the following one to the
same Tune :

SONG

I.

*O*N *Stages Damnation*
 Takes place of Salvation,
Yet our sinful Wretches,
With strange sorts of Fetches,
 Contemn the right Way :
Sons of sound Learning,
Without much Discerning,
You see they do trample
On each good Example ;
 No God will Obey.

II. *Such*

II.

Such base Seducers;
And stubborn Refusers,
For want of Reforming,
　Applaud the rude Times;
They Laugh at, they Scoff at,
　In Derision, Religion,
The greatest of Crimes;
Pimps, Whores, Sharpers, Cullies,
Fools, Panders and Bullies
　Delight in Lewd Rhymes.

III.

Condemning the Motion
Of sincere Devotion,
The Devil has hir'd them
And Furies inspir'd them
　To Ruine the Age:
But if in Season,
You'll know the right Reason,
'Tis hopes to be Damn'd all,
Makes Fellows, who sham all,
　Stand up for the Stage.

IV.

Actors and Ranters,
With Quibbles and Banters,
The Civil War Peal
　Against Piety Ring
But let Hell's Procurers
And all its Insurers
　Forgive, if I Sing,
The Villain that uses
To Ravish the Muses,
　Will Murder his King.

The

The *Play* being done, Hell presently broke Loose ; so Bust-ing thro crowds of Chairmen, Lackies and Coachmen, we got to a Tavern in *Bridges-Street*, which is commonly made a Slaughter-house for Mankind ; where my Company and I sat round a Table, with a Flask of Wine, Pipes, and Tobacco before us, we were got into a deep Discourse concerning what we had seen ; but one a-mong us, (who was so Bewitched with such vain Pastimes, as to make such a Foolish exchange as parting with his Soul for the Transitory Delight of a dangerous Temptation) said, as much Moral Goodness might be Learned at the *Play-house*, as at *Church* ; which most Prophane Expression put me into a great Passion, tell-ing them, that since the Battle between the Archangel and the Dragon, the Devil never found good Harvests till *Stages* were E-rected, on which all the Imorality imaginable is Acted ; insomuch, that whosoever goes there to Learn Good Manners, they may as well go to a *Bawdy-house*, to keep out of Ill Company ; being thoroughly Vex'd, I desir'd them to inform me what Morality was to be Learnt of those, who Grudge one Minute of their time (tho their whole Lives be little enough to prepare for it) in Praying for Heaven, who suffer their Souls to Starve for want of Spiritual Food, and are oftner on their Knees to the Devil, than their God ? In Objection to which, they thought to have silenc'd me, by asking if they could Edify by hearing Persons Preach that, which they Contradicted by their own irregular Lives ; and withal, Reflected on those two unhappy Clergymen, *Foulkes* and *Salisbury*, who were both Executed at *Tyburn*, The first for Murd'ring a Bastard Infant, the other for Counterfeiting Stampt Paper ; but I soon Clencht that Nail on the Head, by letting them know, that if an Unsanctified Minister Preach the Truth, we ought to mind what he delivers in Respect of the Office and Employment he is in, and besides, People ought not to despise such a Man's Doctrine, because our *Saviour* forbids it, *Matt.* 23. 3: Therefore they Swam against the Stream, in Arguing, People might Learn Goodness in a *Play-House*, for if ever any Good Manners was there Taught, it was at the beginning of the *Julian* Period, *Anno* 764: *ante orbem condi-cum* ; then I Requested of them to inform me, what was the Moral of speaking a Prologue on an Ass, by that Fellow who whilst sur-viving, never said Grace, for fear his Breath should Taint the Meat, surely he had but little Skill in *Herauldry*, or else would never put Mettle upon Mettle ; or, what do they Edify to see a Looby Dance the Millar's Dance ; or, what signifies *Cliach* his Mimicking the Cries of Beasts, that have more Sense than himself ; or, what

signifies

signifies the Fencing Master's Vaulting the Horse, any more than a Boy's Vaulting a Post ; or, what signifies it, to see any Logerhead of 'em all, take more care of Traversing his Ground, making a Leg well, and going Gracefully off at an *Exit*, than he doth to perform his Duty to God ? Nothing at all, it signifies no more than a Chip in Porridge towards Morality ; to think of obtaining Heaven by seeing such Vanities, is as insignificant as an illiterate Felon's begging *benefit of the Clergy*, who has not half a Piece to give the *Ordinary* for, for want of it, a *Non Legit* sends him to the place that helps to stock the *Romish* Calendar with Saints, as sure as e're he was Born

These Queries put my Antagonists (so much Bigotted with the Delusions of Plays) to a Non-plus, but to give them the Rising-blow now I had them down, I desir'd to know further what Avail'd towards Good Manners, any Notorious Guinny-dropper's, or Lifeguardsman's Dancing *Cheshire-round* ; or, the Curious performance on a Table by him Stiled, by these Rake-hells, a Gentleman Forsooth ; or, the Sieur *Allard*, and his two Bastards Tumbling like Mad-folks about the Floor ; or Dame *Rayonde* with her Eight Brats Skipping about the Stage ; or, to see any of the Strumpits of the House, impudently shewing their Brawny Calves, when drest in Man's Apparel ; no more towards it, than *William* the Conquerour's *Doomsday-book* : But serviceable perhaps the Ladder-dance may be to some of the *Players*, because if they should come any of them to Die in the Countrey, the same Death as their Brother *Kirkham* did, they are commonly Turn'd off of one there, instead of a Cart ; so not to be ingrateful to the People, who take the Pains to go a Mile or two after them, to see their Behaviour between Heaven and Earth, they may shew them some diverting Tricks, before they leave this World for a Worse. My Opponents being not able to defend the Actors Lewdness, they were for making an Apology in the defence of *Plays* only, Alledging it was a harmless diversion to see *Comedies*, because they innocently set forth the several Love-Toys, and Petty Matters of Men and Women, both Old and Young, as well as Satyrize ill Manners ; which Allegations were but Frivolous Excuses, of wasting precious time to no purpose ; for they may behold how sharply both Ancient and Modern *Satyrists* have Taxed the ill Manners, Bad Lives, and Vices not only of Commons, but even of Kings themselves, which is more edifying to Read off, than to see how they are Acted, the only way to learn Spectators to imitate the like,

as

as *Lactantius* fays, *Spectant hac adolescentes: Quorum lubrica etas, qua franari ac regi debet, ad vitia & peccata hic imaginibus eruditur* : As for *Tragedy*, which Treats of Murders, Exilements, Matters of Grief, Blood and Dirt, they may Read the Stories of them in *Histories*, from whence their Plots are taken; I could fay enough againft the Unlawfulneſs of going to *Plays*; but feeing the Father abovementioned, has done it fufficiently, I refer the Learned Reader to him, *Lib.* 6. *cap.* 20. *te vero cultu.*

O! Times, O! Manners, and a Sinful Age Accurſt! What a pritty way Sinners have found out, to Learn to Efchew a Vice, by feeing Lewdneſs Acted; one Wickedly difpofed, is likely to Reclaim by feeing a Villian Acted; the intreagues of a Town-Miſs; a Bully Flouriſhing his Sword in the Midſt of Twenty God-damn-me's; or, an Infatiate Gilt Cuckolding her Husband; the Wicked I fay again, are likely to Learn Virtue by fuch vain Examples, and efpecially too, being Acted by Women as common as an Inns of Court Privy, and Vagabond Fellows, who Labour to expreſs a deadly Feud betwixt themfelves and their own Souls, and heed no Torments fo much as the Joys of Heaven: Certainly the Spawn of *Players* muft be fome of the Off-fpring of the People of that King who having received a Blow from the hand of God, took a Solemn Oath to be Revenged on him; and Ordained that for Ten Years fpace, no Man fhould Pray to him, or Speak to him; nor fo long as he was in Authority believe in him: *Pliny* in his Natural *History, Lib.* 7. *cap.* 2. Tells of a fort of People that have no Mouths, but Live by the fmell of Herbs, and Flowers, I would to God our *Stage-Players* were fo Born, which might be a let to their Prophane Speaking; but now I think on't again, why do I wiſh this? For if it were fo, they'd make a fhift to be Damn'd, for if they could not Sin by word of Mouth, they would in Thought and Deed; they would Live e'en then as they do now, as if the day of Judgment were paft and gone.

A Good *Chriftian* Detefts to behold fuch Vanities; but had rather go into his Clofet and Weep, for the Miferies a Dying Jefus underwent to Refcue his Soul from the Tyranny of the great *Goliah* of *Hell*, than to go to a *Play-houfe*, to fee a Mimick go a Tip-toe, in Derifion of Mincing Dances, fpeak full Mouthed

D

to Mock the Countrey Clown, or upon the top of the Tongue to Scoff the Citizen, and by their imitating all Ridiculous Gestures or Speeches, in all kind of Vocations, to Provoke his Laughter : Instead of going there, it would be more Conducing to eternal Welfare, if Gentlemen employ'd their time in Reading, Travailing, and Meditation ; the Scholar, like the Bee, gathers Honey from every Flower, Knowledge from every Book he Touches, but most of our Gentry now a Dayes, O ! Scandal to our Countrey, desire to learn no more *Latin*, than what *Lewis* the XI. King of *France* charged his Son to Learn, which was this, *Qui nescit dissimulare, nescit vivere*, He that cannot Dissemble, knows not how to Live : It is beetter for the Soul's good to hear a good Sermon at *Church*, than to hear a wanton Song at the *Theatre*, so called from the *Greek Verb* θιάδαι, i. e. to behold ; and Pray what is it that they behold there ? Nothing but Vanity and Perdition : Wherefore I wish that *Plays* were in as little Estimation with us, as they were when first Play'd in *Rome*, which was then counted infamous to see them, that the Senators and chief People thereof, would not appear where they were Acted.

If *Piety* (as some Wretched Profligates hold) is to be Learned at a *Play-house* as well as at a *Church*, then may we truly stile *Vertue and Vice* Synonimous ; and that we may be sure to Chouse our Souls out of a Future Happiness, cry down *Religion* by calling one a *Religious Man*, as a Term of Debasement, thus lightly do too many in this Vicious Age esteem the Rock of their Salvation : *Tacitus* Annal, *Lib.* 4. Relates that *Stage-Players* were expelled once all out of *Italy*, I wish they were driven out of *England* too ; so severe has the *Church* been against them, that *Lancelotius* in his institution of the *Canon Law*, Writes *Scenicis & Histrionibus non est danda Eucharistia*, that the Sacrament was not to be administred to *Players* ; a Decree made in the first Council of *Orleans* is as Strict, take the Words of it, *De Theatricis, & ipsos placuit, quandiu agunt à communione separari* : My Adversaries having no more to say to these Points discussed, they thought to have silenc'd me, by asking if I could deny but that the *Dramatists*, both Ancient and Modern, had left behind them very good Precepts of Morality in their Writings ; in answer to which Question, I reply'd, that in the Ancient *Greek* and

Latin

Latin Writers of *Drama*'s, there were many excellent Matters
tending to Mrality, but yet they were not so infallible as
to be without Faults, as in that of *Terence* in *Eun.* Act. 3.
Scen. 5. Wherehe brings in *Chœrea* thus idly speaking,

*At quem Deum ! Qui templa cœli summa sonitu concutit, Ego
homuncio hæc non facerem ? Ego illud verò ita feci ac Lubens.*

Which making God his precedent of Debauchery, insinuates
as if he would maintain the Fact to be just, rather than de-
tect the Unlawfulness of it ; a most Reverend *Latin* Father
of the Church finds fault with the same place in these Words :
*Non omnino per hanc turpitudinem verba ista commodius discuntur,
sed per hæc verba turpitudo ista confidentius perpetratur,* Aug. Conf.
Lib. 1. cap. 16. To blame was *Euripides,* in saying,

Rex mundi magna curat ; parva fortuna relinquit ; In which expression he Taxeth God of Partiality ; *absurda est, & impia vox,*
says *Keckerman* of it, *Syst. Theol.* Lib. 1. cap. 7. But no
Marvel it is that such Impiety should proceed from the Mouth
of a *Poet,* that was a secret and concealed *Atheist.* But (take
the Words of Bishop *Fotherby* in his *Atheomastix* Lib. 1. cap.
1.) "Not daring directly to vent out his Atheisme, for fear
'of the Law, devised an Artificial Mean, how to Broach that
'Impiety in another Man's Person, which he durst not in his
'own. And so he Suborned, in his Tragedy, the Person of
'*Sisyphus,* to express all his Ungodliness, and to teach it from
'the Stage : Telling by him a long and formal Tale ; how
'the Life of Men in old time, was like the Life of Beasts ; The
'Stronger, by Violence, Oppressing the Weaker ; until, at last,
'Men were forced to devise severe Laws, for the Repressing of
'such Injustice. But when they found (upon some Tryal)
'that all those Laws could do small Good ; because they could
'only take hold upon such, as were open and publick Offen-
'ces, and not upon Close and Secret ones, there Step'd up
'among them a Subtile Politick Man, who Taught them a
'Mean to provide for that Mischief too ; and to Prevent
'Close Offences, as well as open ones. And that (saith he)
'is this ; if they will but Teach the People, and beat into
'their Heads,

Quod sit perenni vita aliquis vigens Deus,
Qui cernit ista, et audiat, atque intelligat.

Thus fought the *Poet* to teach the People that Impiety from
the *Stage*, which he durst not from the *Pulpit* : And that by
Feigned Person, wnich he durst not in his own. Alas! I coul
Cite Prophane Passages enough, out of the Writings of *Sophocle.*
Aristophanes, Seneca, and *Plautus,* if I went about it, but passin
them by to examine our *English Dramatists,* I shall first call *Shake*
spear to account ; who, in his *Tragedy* call'd *Othello, the Moor*
Venice, instead of presenting that Black General in an humbl
Posture, giving Thanks to Heaven for his great Deliverance fror
a Terrible Storm at Sea, brings him in, Prophanely Complemen
ting his New Betrothed White Wife, in the following Presump
tuous Lines, altogether as Black as his Complexion.

> *O my Soul's Joy,*
>
> *If, after every Tempest, come such Calmness,*
> *May the Winds blow, till they have waken'd Death ;*
> *And let the labouring Bark climb Hills of Seas,*
> *Olympus high, and duck again as low*
> *As Hell's from Heaven.* Act. 2, Scen. 1.

Esquire *Dryden* had a wrong Notion of *Philosophy* in his Head
in these Lines which *Cortez,* in the *Tragedy* call'd the *India*
Emperor, speaks :

> *All things are hush'd, as Nature's Self lay Dead,*
> *The Mountains seem to nod their drowsy Head ;*
> *The little Birds in Dream, their Songs repeat.* Act. 3, Scen.

For where is the Silence so Universal as he talks of, withou
mentioning the Motion of the Mountains, when the Birds ar
all Singing, as Mad as if it were in the Month of *May.*

That was a more Mad than Wise Thought of *Lee,* in hi
Tragedy, call'd, *Theodosius ; Or, the Force of Love,* when he bring
the *Emperor* upon the Stage, newly Converted to the *Christia*
Religion, in a rash Extacy at the sight of *Athenais,* thus pro
phanely speaking ;

Wha

What hinders now, but that, in spight of Rules,
I burst through all the Bands of Death that hold me,
And fly, with such a haste, to that Appearance,
As Bury'd Saints shall make at the last Summons ? Act. 2. Scen. 3.

Truly, this was a hopeful Convert, to make an Article of his Faith a Simile to his Cod-piece Passion : Such Converts as these, I am apt to judge, were not in a much better State of Salvation than *ion of Boristhenes,* who seeing himself near his End, was so afraid of , that he would have endured any Torment rather than Died, and why so ? not so much for the fear of Death it self (tho be very fearful) as because he feared, that after his Death, he should be committed, by God, (whom he had always Defied) into the Hands of the Devil, to be Tormented ; and therefore, at his Dying, he put out his Hand unto him, to bid him Welcome, seeking to Lenify him towards him, with this flattering Salutation, *Salve Pluto, Salve,* Welcome Devil. Welcome.

Truly, the *Play-house* was hard put to it, when they relye upon Women for their Nonsense to support them ; and especially in taking Mrs. *Pix's Farce,* called the *Spanish Wives,* which is stuffed with so much Nonsense, that were I to cite the Faults, I must Incert the whole Work.

Those are mighty edifying Speeches, which *Shadwell,* the Famous Poet Laureat; (in the Second Act of his *Comedy,* call'd the *Humorists*) makes *Drybob* speak about his Dog, *viz. Be-* *sides, this Dog I stole from my Mother, who Lov'd him as well as* *if she had whelp'd him her self :* --- *Madam, I must confess, the Dog* *was not Born in* France, *but of French Parents upon my Honour,* *and is of as ancient a Family, and has as good Blood running in* *his Veins (no dispraise) as e'er a Dog in* France. Indeed, I blush at the Author's Simplicity, of bringing a Person on the Stage, uttering such silly Expressions, that a meer Natural, Lunatick, Half-witted, or Self-conceited Man could not be guilty of Speaking : And of all *Plays,* either *Tragedy, Comedy* or *Farce,* that ever was Written, the only true one was the *Rehearsal,* in which incomparable *Comedy,* the very Fault of insipid *Dramatists,* are exposed to the full.

But again, how moſt intollerably Prophane is their imitating the Works of Nature, as the terrible Meteors of Thunder and Lightning ? Surely, they muſt entertain very low Thoughts of God in ſo doing, or elſe think there is none at all : *Diodorus Siculus*, Lib. 4. tells us, the King of *Elide* uſed to aſtoniſh his People with Artificial Thunder and Lightning, for which Preſumption he was deſtroyed by a Thunderbolt from Heaven : I could tell out of *Stow*, and other Chroniclers, of many that have ſuffer'd in this and other Nations, by Thunder and Lightning, but being confined to Conciſeneſs, I am obliged to omit it. Yet, I muſt needs ſay, that ſuch who have Learning, but Hackney out their Brains, to ſupport an idle Gang of miſocal Raſcals from Starving, they deſerve to be as well Cudgell'd, as *Tom B - - n* was by *Abel R---r*. Our *Engliſh* Dramatiſts (who are all great Plagiaries) put little Morality in their Writings, but Prophaneneſs enough, being as well vers'd in that point of Damnation, as a *Lawyer* is in ſetting People together by the Ears ; wherefore, being ſuch great Bravoes for the Devil, I would adviſe them, in Imitation of *in uſum Delphini*, the ſignifier of thoſe claſſical Scholaſtick Authors, which have the beſt Notes there, to put on the Title-pages of what they Print, *in uſum Diaboli*, as the beſt Books which can direct a down-right Sinner to him : They Live, like *Victuallers*, on the Sins of the People, which verifies the Axiom, *Iiſdem nutritur ex quibus companitur :* They are of the ſame Parentage with good Laws, both extracted out of bad Manners : They are as good at Temporizing, as a *Yorkſhire-Tyke* is at Stealing a Horſe : They hate *Religion*, as bad as a falſe *Scot* does *Epiſcopacy* ; and are ſo often at Difference wit Madam *Pecunia*, that People take care how they invite them to a Feaſt, becauſe they would prove as terrible Slaughter-men, as General *Fairfax's* Officers were wont to be at a Thankſgiving-Dinner.

To conclude, 'tis ſaid, That *Draco's* Laws were Writ in Blood, ſo ſhould we have ſuch againſt the Stage, Writ in the Gore of Actors ; whoſe Bodies and Souls are ſo alike in Sin, that one who never ſaw them in this Life, may Swear them Fellows at the *Reſurrection*. There is a Statute, as you may ſee in *Wingate*, made in the Third Year of King *James* the Firſt, which is this, *None ſhall, in any Stage-Play, Shew, May-game, or Pageant prophanely uſe The Name of God, Chriſt Jeſus, the Holy-Ghoſt, o Trinity, on pain of 10l. to be divided betwixt the King and the Proſe*
cutor

utor : In this Act they were too short, in not providing a-ainst all other Prophaneneſs likewiſe : But I wiſh (as it is likewiſe the wiſh of the greateſt part of the Nation) our pre-ſent wiſe *Senate* will take the Immorality and Prophaneneſs of the *Engliſh Stage,* ſo much into their Conſideration, as to aboliſh it quite ; which Pious Work, to future Ages, would ſtand Recorded for the beſt piece of Service, that ever was done by any Parliament, for the Glory of God, Honour of his Church, and good of all Mankind.

F I N I S

Stage-Plays Arraigned

AND

CONDEMNED;

BY

That Eminent Foreign Theologist,

NAMELY,

WILLIAM AMES,

Doctor and Professor of Divinity of *Francker* in *Friesland*;

IN

A Solution by him given to this following Question,

Quest. *What is to be thought of Stage-Plays?*

LONDON,

Printed, and are to be Sold by *A. Baldwin* in *Warwick-lane*, 1702.

Price 2 *d.*

Stage Plays Arraigned and Condemned, &c.

Queſt. **W**Hat *is to be thought of Stage-Plays ?*

Sol. Such Stage-Plays, as are now in uſe, are utterly to be Condemned : And his Reaſons are theſe.

(1.) They conſiſt in the Lively Repreſentation of Vices and Wickedneſs. And if it be not lawful to name ſuch Vices without deteſtation, [*Eph.* 5. 3.] then certainly much leſs may it be allowed, that the ſame ſhould be expreſſed to the life by Geſtures.

(2.) In the Repreſentation of ſuch Wickedneſſes, the Actors do not only put on the Reſemblance of them, which all Chriſtians ought to abſtain from , [1 *Theſſ.* 5. 22.] but they compoſe themſelves with great care, that they as well conceive them internally, as expreſs ſuch Manners externally. Whence it is, by exerciſing themſelves to it, they diſpoſe themſelves to the ſame Vices ; whence they become ready and prone to execute them without Shame. For , Experience teacheth, that ſome by Acting of Plays have put on

ſuch

such Indecent Habits and Gestures, as they could no
put off again in a long time.

(3.) Some Vices are so represented as they are als
really done, such are *Idle Talk, Ribaldry, Vain Cursing
Execrations,* and the like.

(4.) Either Women are brought upon the Stag
to represent Wantonness with Impudency (who ough
even in the Church to keep Silence) [1 *Cor.* 14. 34.
or to be veiled, [1 *Cor.* 11. 10.] Or Men, for t
please, put on Womens Apparel, Face and Gesture
which is repugnant to the word of God, [*Deut.* 22. 5.
and is a great kindling of Wantonness, and also it give
occasion, and leadeth the right way to those Beastl
nesses which are against Nature. *Rom.* 1. 27.

(5.) Both Actors and Spectators seek delight i
those things, of which they ought to be ashamed
Rom. 6. 21.

(6.) They expose themselves to manifest hazard
For they, which are most modest, can hardly avoid th
Tickling Thoughts of unlawful things, and other
learn to do that which they were wont to hear an
see without Blushing. The wiser of the Ethnicks them
selves did observe this, amongst whom *Seneca : Nothin
is more dangerous to good manners, than to set at a Shew
for then Vices creep in more easily by Pleasure.*

(7.) If there be any of so hard a Breast, that the
are not moved with such Sights, yet they give Scanda
to others, who by their Example are drawn into dan
gers and sins.

(8.) Grea

(5)

(8.) Great Cost is vainly, and with hurt bestowed. For, with the Charges that are laid upon one Stage-Play, many Poor may be sustained some Months.

(9.) Stage-Players by the Civil Law are Infamous. In the Primitive Church they were excluded from the Ecclesiastical Communion.

(10.) In times past it was a Solemn Vow of all, that were Baptized : *I renounce the Devil, his Pomps and Works, from whence* Salvian de provid. Lib. 6. *doth thus discourse : In all Spectacles there is a certain Apostacy of the Faith, and a deadly prævarication from the Symbols and Heavenly Sacraments of it. For what is the first Confession of Christians in saving Baptism ? What else, but that they profest to renounce the Devil, his Pomps, Shews and Works ? Therefore Spectacles and Pomps, according to our Profession, are the Works of the Devil. How canst thou, O Christian, after Baptism follow Shews, which thou confessest to be the work of the Devil ? Thou hast once renounced the Devil and his Shews : And by this thou must necessarily know, that when willingly, and upon Knowledge thou dost go again to Plays, thou returnest to the Devil ; for thou hast renounced both together, and didst account one as both : If thou returnest to one, thou hast gone back to both. For thou sayest I Renounce the Devil, his Pomps, Shews and Works. And what then, I do believe (thou sayst) in God the Father,* &c. *Therefore the Devil is first Renounced, before God is believing, because he which doth not Renounce the Devil, doth not believe in God. And therefore he which returneth to the Devil, leaveth God. The Devil is in his Shews and Pomps, and by this when we return to Spectacles, we leave the Faith of Christ.* So Holy *Salvian* out of

B   *Ter-*

Tertullian (as it seemeth) *de Spectac.* c. 4. *& de Idolat.* c. 6. where the like sayings are found.

Those Objections and Limitations, which are brought by some Divines in favour of these Plays, are of no moment.

Object. It is Objected first, That Stage-Players are some way necessary. For seeing that Recreation is necessary to man, and nothing doth recreate and delight more than such kind of Sports, it followeth, that they are necessary.

Answ. 1. Lawful Recreations or Sports do consist in things indifferent, which are neither appointed, nor forbidden by God. For we ought not to use forbidden Things, and it is not lawful to rest with Precepts. But it hath been proved before, that Stage-Plays do consist in things forbidden.

2dly, Those delights, which either spring from things unlawful, or which give an occasion to things unlawful, are vicious and deadly.

3dly, The too much inticings to carnal Pleasures ought to be avoided, and suspected as dangerous as if they were snares : Because they make the Flesh wanton, and infect, and press down the Mind. And truly, there is no other cause, why common Stage-Plays do so much tickle the multitude, than that they are bathed in all filthy pleasure by them, from the Image of those Lusts which they love, by any means to nourish and stir up in themselves.

Ob-

Object. It is Objected fecondly, that there is a manifold profit of thefe fports, becaufe they help the underftanding and memory, in the knowledge of things ; they promote the Flight of Vice, and Love of Vertue, and render both Speech and Manners more neat and civilized.

Anfw. 1. If thefe were means, which brought fo much profit, without doubt they would have fome approbation in the Word of God. But others, and not thefe means are allowed of in the Word of God, by the ufe of which thofe perfections ought to be attained.

2dly, Such means are wont to be fanctified to Chriftians by the Word and Prayer. [1 *Tim.* 4. 5.] But is altogether unheard of, and ftrange to the nature of thefe fports, that one fhould prepare himfelf by Prayer to the ufe of them.

3dly, Experience of all Ages fheweth, and the Manners of Stage-Players do proclaim it, that the Underftanding, and Memory are polluted by fuch Sports, Vices promoted, and Virtues extinguifhed.

Object. It is Objected, thirdly, that thofe Sports may have an honeft end, a laudable Subject, as a Hiftory of the Bible, and honeft Actors, free from lightnefs and fcurrility.

Anfw. 1. When the end of the deed is difhoneft, it cannot be made honeft by the intention of the doer.

2dly,

2dly, If choice of the two were to be granted, it seemeth more sufferable, that Prophane rather than Sacred Stories should be acted by Players. For the Majesty of the Word of God, which ought to be heard, and thought on, with fear and trembling, is debased, spoiled, and abused in an unworthy manner, if it be turned into a matter of sport.

3dly, If Lightness and Scurrility be taken from the Scene, the common Stage itself is likewise taken away ; because it will be destitute of Actors and Spectators. The Heathen Philosopher observed this of old *Tusc. Quæst.* lib. 4. *Poetry, the most famous correctness of Life, which thinks it fit, that the Lover of Vices, and Author of Levity, should be placed in the Council of the Gods. I speak of Comedy, which except we did allow of these offences, would not be at all.* Doctor *Ames* in his Cases of Conscience, lib. 5. cap. 39. of *Immodest Luxury*, question 7. With which learned Author do concur in the same opinion, against Interludes, and Stage Plays, M. *Frid. Windelinus* in his Tract of Moral Philosophy, *lib.* 1. *c.* 19. *Quest.* 6. The Lord Arch-bishop *Usher*, in his Body of Divinity, Pag. 280. Edit. 1648. and Doctor *Rivet* in his Explication of the Decalogue, pag. 339.

F I N I S.

AN
Humble Application
TO THE
QUEEN,

And Her Great Council,

THE

Parliament of *England*,

To SUPPRESS

Play-Houses and *Bear-Baitings*,

With All

Prophaness and *Immorality*.

By John Feild.

*For Rulers are not a Terror to Good Works, but to Evil.—But if
thou do that which is Evil, be afraid; for he beareth not the
Sword in vain: For he is the Minister of God, to revenge
Wrath upon him that doth Evil,* Rom. 13. 3, 4.

LONDON, Printed and Sold by T. Sowle, in *White-
Hart-Court* in *Gracious-Street*, 1703.

AN
Humble Application
TO THE
QUEEN,
And Her Great Council, the
Parliament of *England*, &c.

IN Humility I make this Application to the QUEEN, and Her Great Council, the Parliament : That they would, in the Fear and Wisdom of God, be pleased, for his Honour, the Good of the Nation, and Reputation of the Christian Religion, not to License or Countenance, with Authority, any *Play-Houses, Revellings* at the *Temple, Dice-playing, Gaming, Stage-Players, Bull or Bear-baitings,* but totally to suppress and put them down ; for thereby *Vice, Prophaness, Debauchery* and *Immorality,* do greatly abound, and are so Provokingly Practised, to the Scandal of Religion, and Ruine of many. And that Effectual Care may be also taken, that no *Cursing, Swearing,* or Calling upon God to *Damn their Souls,* may be Practised or Indulged by any, especially *Legislators,* or those that are in any Publick Stations or Imployments in the Government; that so all which are under them, may, by their Sober Carriage, and Exemplary Conversations, be brought to Shame, and inclined to Repentance, and Amendment of their Lives and Practices; that so the Lord may turn away his Wrath, and the Blessings of God may be Enjoyed and Continued to this Nation.

For is not this the End, for which the *most High God,* that

Rules

Rules in the *Kingdoms of Men*, and appointeth over it whom-soever he will, (the God in whose Hand the Breath of all Living is) hath, by his *Divine Providence*, placed the present QUEEN upon the Throne of Her *Royal Ancestors*? And is it not by the Lord, *Power* is given unto Her, and *Sovereignty* from the Highest?.

And as She bears Rule among Men, it's my Hearty Desire and Prayer unto God, she may be Just; *Ruling in the Fear of God*; that so she may be Endued with that Wisdom, by whom *Kings reign, and Princes decree Justice*, and may not Bear the Sword in Vain; but be a *Terror* to them that do Evil, and a *Praise* to them that do well; that Her Throne may be Established in *Righteousness*, and the *Blessings of God* may be upon Her and her People; and that she may *Live for ever*.

And I am the more Emboldned thus to make my Humble Application to the *Queen* and the *Parliament*, and have the more ground to hope this my Request will be answered by Her and Them, Because she hath, in Her Royal Proclamation, *For the Encourage-ment of Piety and Vertue, and Preventing and Punishing of Vice, Pro-phaness and Immorality*, dated the 26th of *March*, 1702. Thus declared to Her Subjects, viz.

' We most Seriously and Religiously Considering, that
' it is an Indispensible Duty on Us, to be Careful, above
' all other Things, to Preserve and Advance the Honour
' and Service of Almighty God, and to Discourage and
' Suppress All Vice, Prophaness, Debauchery and Immo-
' rality; which are so highly Displeasing to God, so great
' Reproach to our Religion and Government, and (by means
' of the frequent ill Examples of the Practicers thereof) have
' so fatal a Tendency, to the Corruption of many of our
' Loving Subjects, otherwise Religiously and Vertuously
' Disposed, and which (if not timely Remedied) may
' justly draw down the Divine Vengeance upon Us, and
' Our Kingdoms.

Is there not therefore great need, in *Duty to God*, to Advance his *Honour*, and Prevent his *Vengeance*, and take away Reproach from our *Religion* and *Government*; that those *Nurseries of Vice*, the *Play-Houses*, *Stage-Players*, *Revellings* and *Gaming*, with *Bull* and *Bear-baitings*, may be totally Suppressed and put down, which have so great and fatal a Tendency, to the Corruption of the Queen's Subjects, and Ruine of many; and may draw down

(as.

(as such Provoking Abominations often have) the *Divine Vengeance*, if continued; as she well and truly observes, saying:

' We humbly acknowledge, We cannot expect the Bles-
' sing and Goodness of Almighty God (by whom Kings and
' Queens Reign, and on which we intirely Rely) to make
' our Reign happy and Prosperous to our Self and People,
' nor hope for the Divine Assistance to Deliver us from the
' Great and Eminent Dangers, which our Kingdom, and
' the true Protestant Religion established among Us, are in
' this present Juncture threatned with, without a Religious
' Observance of God's Holy Law.

I therefore hope, the *Queen* and *Parliament* will Actually put down all *Play-Houses*, and not suffer *Stage-Players*, and *Riotous Meetings* at *Bear-Gardens*, &c. to be upheld, under Pretence of her *Authority*, nor so to be Published in Print unto the World, as is too common by the *Holders* thereof: Inasmuch as the *Queen*, by the Advice of her *Privy Council*, doth declare thus;

' It is our Royal Purpose and Resolution, to Discounte-
' nance and Punish all manner of Vice and Immorality in
' All Persons, and Every Degree or Quality, within this
' Realm; and particulary in such that are Imployed near
' our Royal Person: And that for the greater Incourage-
' ment of Religion and Morality, We will, upon all occa-
' sions, distinguish Persons of Piety and Vertue, by Marks
' of our Royal Favour.

Wherefore it may be humbly hoped, that the *Queen* and her *Parliament*, will not only openly declare against, but put down these manifest *Provocations*, as they desire her *Reign* may be *Prosperous*, and hope for *Divine Assistance* and *Deliverance*, from those Great and Eminent Dangers, which the *Queen*, her *Nation*, and *Protestant Religion*, are threatned with.

For most certain it is, as the late *King*, the *Queen*'s Royal Brother, did declare in his *Proclamation*, dated the 24th of *February*, 1697. viz.
' Nothing can prove a greater Dishonour to a Well-ordered Go-
' vernment, where the Christian Faith is Professed, nor is likelier
' to Provoke God to withdraw his Mercy and Blessings from us,
' and instead thereof, to inflict heavy and severe Judgments upon
' this Kingdom, than the open and avowed Practice of Vice, Im-
' morality and Prophaness, which amongst Men has too much
' prevailed in this our Kingdom of late Years, to the high Displeasure

'pleasure of Almighty God, the great Scandal of Christianity,
'and the ill and fatal Example of the rest of our Loving Sub-
'jects, who have been Soberly Educated, and whose Inclinations
'would lead them to the Exercise of Piety and Vertue, did they
'not daily find such frequent and repeated Instances of Dissolute
'Living, Prophaness and Impiety.

Also the late Queen *Mary*, in her *Letter* (in the absence of the
King) *to the Justices of the Peace in the County of* Middlesex, *for the
Suppressing of Prophaness and Debauchery,* dated *July 9. 1691.* saith,
'*Concerning the Great and Indispensible Duty incumbent upon
'Us, to Promote and Encourage a Reformation of the Manners
'of all Our Subjects ; that so the Service of God may be Ad-
'vanced, and those Blessing be Procured to these Nations, which
'always attend a Consciencious Discharge of Our Respective Du-
'ties, according to our several Relations : We think it necessary,
'in order to the Obtaining of this Publick Good, to Recommend
'to you the putting in Execution, with all Fidelity and Impar-
'tiality, those Laws which have been made, and are still in
'force, against the Profanation of the Lord's Day, Drunken-
'ness, Prophane Swearing and Cursing, and all other Lewd,
'Enormous, and Disorderly Practices,——for preventing of such
'Judgments which are Solemnly Denounced against the Sins
'above-mentioned,——as you tender the Honour of Almighty God,
'the Flourishing Condition of his Church in this Kingdom, the
'Continuance of his Holy Religion among Us, and the Pro-
'sperity of your Country.*

And the House of Commons, in their Address to the late King
William, well observed : '*The Examples of Men in High and
'Publick Stations, have a Powerful Influence upon the Lives
'of others ; (and therefore say) We do most humbly Beseech
'your Majesty, That all Vice, Prophaness and Irreligion,
'may in a particular manner be Discouraged, in all those
'who have the Honour to be Employed near your Royal
'Person, and in all others who are in your Majesty's Ser-
'vice, by Sea and Land ; appointing strict Orders to be
'given

given to all your Commanders, That they not only shew a good Example themselves, but also inspect the Manners of those under them : And that your Majesty would, upon all occasions, distinguish Men of Piety and Vertue, by Marks of your Royal Favour.

And that noted Book, Intituled, *An Account of the Societies for Reformation of Manners*, &c. printed 1699. *Which hath been Perused and Recommended, the Design of which is so truly Great and Noble, so much for the Honour of God, the Advancement of Piety and Vertue, and the Publick Good both of Church and State, that it cannot fail of being approved by all good Men*, as the Twenty Nine Temporal Lords, Nine Bishops, and Seven Judges, declared to the Author ; see the Book. And in page 4. of the said Book : ' It's well observed, that in our *open Streets*, as if we were resolved to out-do the *Impieties* of the very *Heathens, Prophaness,* and even *Blasphemy,* was too often the Wit and Entertainment of our Scandalous Play-Houses, and *Sincere Religion* became the Jest and Scorn of our Courts in the late Reigns. And thus Debauchery diffused it self throughout the whole Body of the Nation, till at last our Morals were so Corrupted, that *Vertue* and *Vice* had with too many changed their Names : It was reckoned *Breeding* to *Swear, Gallantry* to be *Lewd, Good Humour* to be *Drunk,* and *Wit* to despise *Sacred Things ;* and it was enough to have rendred one suspected of *Phanaticism,* or an Abjectness of Spirit, and a Matter of Reproach, not to suffer one's self to be carried away with the *Torrent of Wickedness,* and not to glory in those *Fashionable Vices.*

Thus we see, we have *Three Crowned Heads,* the *Parliament* of *England, Twenty Nine Lords, Nine Bishops,* and *Seven Judges,* Testifying against *Vice* and *Immorality.*

Therefore it's humbly Requested, That the *Government* would be pleased totally to Suppress all the *Play-Houses,* that none of them may be suffered to pretend the *Queen's Authority* or *License* or any of them ; being the *Nurseries* of *Debauchery,* the *Bane* of *Youth,* the *Corruption of Manners,* and the *Shame* of *Government,* and *Scandal* of *Christianity :* ' That *Religion* be not treated (as saith the aforesaid Book, p. 114.) ' with any Disrespect ; particularly, that it be not made the Scorn of any Order or Body of Men, the common Subject of the Prophane Play-Houses, or the Sport of Buffoons ; and that the open Violation of it, by Prophane
' Swearing

' Swearing and Curfing, Drunkenneſs, Lewdneſs, &c. be fup-
' preſſed; as all Wiſe Nations, I conceive, have ever done, and
' ever will do.

I hope it will not be either Offenſive or Improper, to add to
the foregoing Quotations, ſomething farther on the ſame Subject,
and agreeable thereto, out of Hiſtrio Maſtix, the Players Scourge,
or Actor's Tragedy ; by which it appears, the Author was an
Antiquary of great Reading and Induſtry on this Subject; ſhew-
ing, Magiſtrates, Emperors and Princes, have Excluded, Suppreſſed,
and Condemned Stage-Plays : And in pag. 713, 714, 715. ſaith,
' If we look upon Heathen States or Nations, we ſhall find the
' Ancient Lacedemonians, Athenians, Grecians, Romans, Germans,
' Maſcilienſes, Goths and Vandals ; if upon Heathen Magiſtrates,
' Emperors or Princes, we ſhall ſee Licurgus, Solon, Plato, Socrates,
' Themiſtocles, Scipio, Naſſica, Trebonius, Rufinus, Junius Mauricus,
' together with Auguſtus Cæſar, Tiberius, Nero, Trajan, Marcus
' Aurelius, Domitian, Julian, and the whole Roman Senate, Exclu-
' ding, Suppreſſing, Condemning Plays and Actors, as the occaſion
' of much Vice and Lewdneſs, the Fomenters of Whoredoms, Ef-
' feminacy, Idleneſs, &c. the Corrupters of the Peoples Minds and
' Manners, the Authors of many Tumults, Diſcords, Diſorders ;
' the Cauſes of much Prodigality, of many Intolerable Miſchiefs
' in a State.——If we look on Chriſtian States or Nations, we ſhall
' diſcern the whole State and Nation of the Jews, both before
' and ſince Chriſt's time, together with all the Primitive Chri-
' ſtians, the Waldenſes, Albingenſes, and French Proteſtants, the Cities
' of Geneva, Tigure, Baſil, and the whole State of England, in ſundry
' Acts of Parliament, Condemning, Suppreſſing Plays and Players,
' as moſt Prophane Unchriſtian Spectacles, not Tolerable in any
' Chriſtian Republick.——' If we deſire any Precedents of Chri-
' ſtian Emperors, Princes, Magiſtrates, we have not only the Ex-
' amples of Noah, Melchizedec, Abraham, Iſaac, Jacob, Joſeph,
' Moſes, Joſhua, David, Solomon, Hezekiah, Joſiah, with other Godly
' Patriarchs, Kings and Princes, Recorded in the Scriptures for
' our Chriſtian Imitation ; who were ſo far from Cheriſhing,
' from Approving, Enterludes, Mummeries, Maſques, or Stage-Plays,
' either in their Palaces, Courts, or Kingdoms, (as too many
' Princes ſince have done) that we never Read in Scripture, nor
' in any other Story whatſoever, that they were ſo much at
' once Experimentally Acquainted with them : The whole Jewiſh
Nation

'Nation (some few Apostates only excepted) Oppugning them
'from time to time (and so by Consequence, these Patriarchs,
'Magistrates, and Princes too.) as Opposite to their *Religion,*
'*Manners, Laws,* and *Government* : —— (Which methinks should
'somewhat move. all Christian Princes and Governments, to
'abandon *Stage-Plays* now ; since they can find no King, no
'Pious Person, in all the *Bible,* that ever harboured or beheld
'them heretofore) But likewise the Patterns of *Constantine, Theo-*
'*dosius, Leo, Anthemius, Justinian, Valentinian, Valens, Gratian,*
'*Charles* the Great, *Theodoricus, Henry* the Third Emperor of that
'Name, *Philip Augustus* King of *France,* our Famous Queen *Eli-*
'*zabeth,* and her *Council,* with our *London Magistrates* and *Uni-*
'*versities* in her Reign ; who all Suppressed, Inhibited *Stage-*
'*Plays, Sword-Plays* and *Actors,* as Unsufferable Mischiefs in any
'Christian State or City. To these I might add *Ludovicus* the
'Emperor, who, by his publick Edicts, agreeing *Verbatim* with
'the Seven and Eight fore-quoted Canons of *Synodus Turonensis,*
'p. 589, 590. Inhibited all *Ministers,* all *Clergy-Men,* from *Stage-*
'*Plays, Hunting, Hauking,* &c. Together with *Charles* the Ninth,
'and *Henry* the Third of *France* ; who by their Solemn *Laws* and
'*Edicts,* prohibited all *Stage-Plays,* all *Dancing on Lords Days,* or
'other *solemn Annual Festivals,* under Pain of Imprisonment, and
'other Penalties, to be Inflicted by the Magistrates : And our
'own most Gracious Soveraign Lord King *Charles,* who, together
'with the *whole Court of Parliament,* in the First Year of his
'Highnesses Reign, Enacted this most Pious Play-Condemning
'Law, Intituled, *An Act for Prohibiting of divers Abuses commit-*
'*ted on the Lord's Day, called Sunday* : *Forasmuch as there is no-*
'*thing more acceptable to God, than the true and sincere Worship of*
'*him, according to his Holy Will* ; *that the holy keeping the Lord's*
'*Day, is a principal part of the true Worship of God, which in very*
'*many places of this Realm, hath been, and now is, prophaned and*
'*neglected, by a Disorderly sort of People, in Exercising and Frequent-*
'*ing* Bear-baiting, Bull-baiting, **Enterludes, Common Plays,**
'*and other Unlawful Exercises and Pastimes.*
'P. 717. If then all these Pagan, these Christian Nations, Re-
'publicks, Emperors, Princes, Magistrates, have thus abandoned,
'censured, suppressed *Plays* and *Players,* out of a long Experimental
'Knowledge of their many vicious lewd Effects: Or are we ashamed
'to be like our Ancestors, in Judgment, in Opinion, as we are in

'Tonsure,

'Tonsure, Complement, Habit and Attire, in this *Age of Novel-*
'*ties,* which likes of Nothing that is old or common, *(though*
'*such things commonly are best of all)* that we thus undervalue the
'Resolutions of all former Ages, in this Case of *Plays* and *Players,*
'preferring our own Wits and Lusts before them? O let us be
'ashamed now, at last to Countenance, to Plead for that, which
'the very best, the wisest Heathens, yea, Christian Nations, States
'and Magistrates, of all sorts, have thus branded, and cast out,
'as Lewd, as Vicious, as Abominable, in the very highest degree:
'And let us now submit our Judgments, our Practice, Lusts, and
'Foolish Fancies, to their deliberate, mature, experimental Cen-
'sures; Abominating, Condemning *Plays* and *Players,* if not Exiling
'them our Cities, Coasts and Country, as all these have done;
'Arming our selves with peremptory Resolutions against all fu-
'ture *Stage-Players.*

And in his *Epistle Dedicatory* the 2d. to shew what's said is no Ficti-
ous *Novelty,* or Conceited *Singularity,* he saith, 'It hath the Concur-
'rent Testimony, the Unanimous Resolution, of sundry Texts of
'Scripture, of the whole Primitive Church and Saints of God,
'both before and under the Law and Gospel, the Canons of
'Fifty Five several Oecumenical, National, Provincial Synods
'and Councils, of divers Ages and Countries; together with the
'Canonical, the Imperial Constitutions of the Apostles them-
'selves, of Emperors, Popes, and other Bishops, the Works
'of Seventy One Fathers, and Ancient Christian Writers, of
'Chiefest Note, from our Saviour's Nativity, to the Year 1200.
'the Suffrages of above One Hundred and Fifty Christian Au-
'thors, of all sorts, from the Year 1200. to this present; the
'Sentence of Forty Heathen Philosophers, Orators, Historians,
'Poets; together with the Play-Condemning Laws and Edicts
'of sundry Christian, yea, Pagan Nations, Republicks, Emperors,
'Princes, Magistrates, in several Ages; with the Statutes, Ma-
'gistrates, Universities, Writers and Preachers of our own Re-
'nowned Kingdom, to back, to second them in all particulars;
'who have long since passed this heavy Censure against Stage
'Plays, That they are the very Works, the Pomps, Inventions,
'and chief Delights of the Devil, which all Christians solemnly
'Abjure in their Baptism, the most pestilent Corruption of all
'Men's, (especially Young Men's) *Minds* and *Manners;* the chief
'Fomenters of all *Vice* and *Wickedness;* the greatest Enemies o

'al

all *Vertue*, *Grace* and *Goodness*: the most mischievous Plagues that can be harboured in *Church* or *State*; yea, Lewd, Infernal Pastimes, not Tolerable among Heathens, not Sufferable in *any* well-ordered Christian Republick; not once to be haunted or applauded by any Civil Vertuous Persons, who are either mindful of their Credits, or of their own Salvation: Which, as it controls the gross Mistake of divers Voluptuous, Paganizing Christians in our Days, who dote on Stage-Plays, as the most Laudable, Generous, if not Necessary Recreations, so it should now at last Engage all Christians for ever to abandon them, as the very best of Saints, of Pagans, have done in former Ages. Alas, what Goodness, what Profit do Men reap from *Stage-Plays*, that should any ways Engage their Affections to them? Do they not *Enrage* their Lusts, *Add* Fire and Fewel to their Unchaste Affections, *Deprave* their Minds, *Corrupt* their Manners, *Cauterize* their Consciences, *Obdurate* their Hearts, *Multiply* their heinous Transgressions, *Consume* their Estates, *Misspend* their Time, *Canker* their Graces, *Blast* all their Vertues, *Interrupt* their Studies, *Indispose* them to Repentance, and true Godly Sorrow for their Sins; make all God's Ordinances ineffectual to their Spiritual Good; draw down the Guilt of sundry Play-House-Abominations on their Persons; Incorporate them into Lewd and Ungodly Company; and, without Repentance, Damn their Souls? Do they not Dishonour their most Holy God, Abuse their most Blessed Saviour sundry ways, Blaspheme and Grieve God's Holy Spirit, Prophane the Sacred Scriptures, and the Name of God; Deride and Jeer Religion, Holiness, Vertue, Temperance, Grace, Goodness, with all Religious Vertuous Persons; Advance the Devil's Sceptre, Service, Kingdom, by Sowing, by Cherishing the Seeds of *Atheism*, *Heathenism*, *Prophaness*, *Incontinency*, *Voluptuousness*, *Idleness*, yea, all kind of *Wickedness*, in their Actors and Spectators Hearts.

And it's my Hearty Desire to God, That all *Just* and *Pious* Inclinations and Resolutions in the QUEEN, may be Effectually put in *Practice*; and the Eminent Dangers, which her Kingdom, and true Protestant Religion, are in this Juncture threatned with, *prevented*; and the heavy and severe Judgments of God, *Diverted*; and the Dishonour of the Christian Religion Professed, *Removed*; God's Holy Law *Observed*, the Blessings of God *Enjoyed*, and the QUEEN's Reign made *Prosperous*, and Her Subjects *Happy*.

A.

A Brief Cautional Conclusion, more Generally respecting a Spiritual and Inward Reformation.

AS the true Intent of *Magistracy*, being a *Divine Ordinance*, is for the *Punishment* and *Terror of Evil-doers*, and *Praise of them that do well*; and, so far as their Power extends, to work an *outward Reformation* from manifest *Wickedness*, and gross *Provocations* : So it is the Work of *Christ*, by his *Light*, *Grace*, and good *Spirit*, to work an Inward and Effectual *Reformation* in *Peoples Hearts*; and as *Soveraign Lord* over the Conscience, to bring them to *keep a Conscience void of Offence towards God, and all Men*: For it is He only, that *searcheth the Heart*, can work this *Inward Reformation*, which doth Remove the Occasion of these *Outward Laws* and *Penalties*, which were added because of *Transgression*.

I therefore do earnestly desire, That all, who Believe there is a God, and profess Faith in Him, and his dear Son, the Lord Jesus Christ; and own the Holy Spirit, that proceeds from the *Father* and the *Son*, and is *poured forth in this day upon all Flesh, according to God's Promise*, may Receive and Learn thereof; that thereby all may not only Know what is *Good*, and what their *Duty* is towards *God*; but be Enabled to the Faithful *Performance*, and Sincere *Discharge* thereof : It's for that end, God (that requires us to *Love*, *Fear*, and *Serve* Him) hath been pleased to bestow it upon All, that so they may be Enabled to *do his Will*, and in neglect thereof, be left without *Excuse* in the Great *Day of Account*. For had he given Man a *Law* and *Command*, and not afforded him that which was sufficient to Abilitate him to *keep* and *observe* the same, Man might have some Excuse; but it is not so, and therefore he *justly* Punishes them that do not keep his holy *Law* and *Command*.

It's very observable in Holy Writ, and ought Seriously to be Considered by all that own the Divine Authority thereof, That ever since the *great Creator of all Things*, the *most High God*, made Man in his own *Image* of *Righteousness*, and gave to him his *holy Law* and *Command*, that the Breach and Violation thereof by Man hath been the Cause of all the great Calamities and severe Judgment

Judgments, which the Righteous God hath brought upon the Children of Men, in the several Ages of the World, unto this Day : Some of which, this Nation, and other parts of the *Queen's* Dominions, have been large Sharers of, by *Pestilence*, *Wars*, *Fire*, and particularly *Famine* in *Scotland*, not many Years since.

For Prevention of which, for the future, I humbly Pray Almighty God, *that hath the Hearts of all Men in his Hand*; That He would turn every one, both High and Low, from the Evil of their Ways, and Abomination of their Doings, and Incline their Hearts to keep his *Law*, and bring them to Learn of his *Grace*, which appears unto them, (and came by Jesus Christ, his dear Son, whom all ought to hear and obey) that they may be taught, not only to *deny all Ungodliness*; but through his Sufficient Grace, may be enabled to *refrain* from, and *abandon* all *Vice*, *Prophaness* and *Immorality*, whatsoever ; and may come, by his holy Spirit, to know their Hearts, and all their Members, mortified from all Worldly and Carnal Lusts ; that they may, in all things, obey his Blessed Will, through the same, his dear Son Jesus Christ.

Now the Way for a General *Reformation of Manners*, and *Amendment of Life*, is for every one, of what *Rank*, *Quality*, or *Degree* soever, to Love and Learn of that *Spirit*, *Grace* and *Truth*, that is come by *Christ*, and to Believe in him ; for then will they truly know *God* to be their *Father*, *Christ* their *Saviour*, and this *Holy Spirit* their *Sanctifier*, from all *Vicious*, *Prophane*, *Immoral*, *Ungodly Ways* and *Practices*, and *Dissolute Living* : And so to avoid that, which not only the *Queen*, her *Royal Predecessors*, the *Parliament*, the *Twenty Nine Lords*, *Nine Bishops*, and *Seven Judges* by Name, have Cautioned against, and Discountenanced ; but all that also, which is *highly* Displeasing, and *greatly* Provoking to *Almighty God*.

Let not therefore any, *High* or *Low*, think it's enough to Testify against these *Abominations*, and to say within themselves, They have *God* to their *Father*, *Christ* for their *Saviour*, the *Holy Ghost* for their *Sanctifier*, and that they Believe therein, and Profess the *Christian Religion*, and *dislike* these things ; and yet either *Continue* therein, or *Connive* thereat, and *Encourage* or *Countenance* (by their own *Example)* such, or any of these *Evils* : For thereby they will the more Provoke *God*, Incur his *Displeasure*, Scandalize the *Christian Religion*, and Contract the greater *Guilt* upon their own *Souls*. And if they forsake not their *Sins*, and unfeignedly Repent
pent

pent thereof, and amend their Ways, and put away the Evil of their Doings from before the Eyes of Him, that Knows their *Thoughts*, Records their *Actions*, and will most certainly bring *every Work to Judgment*, with *every Secret Thing*, and Reward every one according to their Works; and those that live in, and love their Evil Ways, and dye in their Sins and Unbelief, shall know a being *Punished with Everlasting Destruction from the Presence of the Lord, and Glory of his Power, for ever*; and have their Portion in *Eternal Misery*, where the *Worm never dyeth*, nor the *Fire never goes out*; where there is *Weeping, Wailing, and Gnashing of Teeth, for ever and ever*.

Therefore it's my Tender Counsel and Advice, in the Love of Him, *that would have all Men to be saved*; and in the Love of Him, *that Died for every Man, and Rose again*; That every one, whilst they have time here, (which is both short and uncertain) would mind the *inward Convictions*, and *secret Reproofs*, of that Spirit, which Christ said, *shall Convince the World of Sin*; *A Manifestation of which Spirit is given to every one to profit withal*; and whosoever have not this Spirit, are no true Christians; nor can any be the *Children, or Sons of God*, but those that are *Born of*, and *Led by this Holy Spirit*; neither can any be *Led into all Truth*, but by this Spirit; nor have a *part in Christ*, unless they be Washed and Sanctified thereby.

Therefore I earnestly Intreat all, That these things might have their *due Weight*, and *deliberate Consideration*; and that there may be a *hearty* and *sincere* Desire, to Answer the *Law of God*, to Keep his *holy Commands*, to Discharge our *Duty* to Him, to *Love, Fear*, and *Serve* Him, to know *Peace* with him, to *Enjoy* his Blessing, to *Honour* his dear Son, the Lord *Jesus Christ*, to Observe his *Doctrine*, to Answer our *Christian Profession*, to make the holy Scriptures our *Rule of Faith* and *Practice*; which say, *Finally Brethren, whatsoever things are True, whatsoever things are Honest, whatsoever things are Just, whatsoever things are Pure, whatsoever things are Lovely, whatsoever things are of good Report; if there be any Vertue, and if there be any Praise, think on these things*; for they certainly are such that Christians ought to follow.

And if the Nation expect *God's Blessings*, and that his severe *Judgments* should be Averted, let not those things, that are neither *Honest, Just, Pure, Lovely*, or of *good Report*, that have no *Vertue* or *Praise* in them, be practised, given way to, or fre-

quented

quented by any, as *Stage-Plays*, *Bull* and *Bear-baitings*, *Drolleries*, *Comedies*, *Tragedies*, *Dicing*, *Revellings*, *Drunkenness*, or any *Vice* or *Immoralities* whatsoever; for they are contrary to the *Law* and *Commands* of God, the *Mind of Christ*, the *Doctrine* of the *Christian Religion*, and ought therefore to be carefully and diligently avoided, by all that make Profession thereof, and have any regard to the Good of their Souls; for no Enormities ought to be Countenanced or Tolerated by *Christian Governours*, but Excluded, Censured, and totally Suppressed; as I humbly hope the *Queen*, and her *Parliament* will, that they may prevent, what in them lies, all those Disorders and Disorderly sort of People, Exercising themselves in such things, and Frequenting *Play-Houses*, *Bear-baitings*, *Bull-baitings*, &c. And if all would receive and learn of the *Spirit* and *Grace of God* in their own Hearts, they would be taught to deny all *Vice*, *Immorality* and *Prophaness* whatsoever; and then the *Christian Religion* would appear in its Lustre, and the Professors thereof, would in Life, Practice and Conversation, *shine in their several Stations*; so that others *seeing their good Works*, might glorifie God in their Behalf. And the way for this *General Reformation* to be throughly Effected, is, as I have said, for all to Receive and Live in the *Spirit of Christ*, whom they Profess, and to Walk therein; for then they shall not fulfil the *Lusts of the Flesh*, nor be found in any of the *Works thereof*, which Offend God, Dishonour his *Holy Name*, and are a Scandal to the true *Christian Religion*, and Grieve *God's Holy Spirit*, and bring *Death* and *Damnation* upon them that *live* and *die* therein.

Oh therefore! that every one, that Professes *Faith* in *God*, and in our Lord *Jesus Christ*, and in his *Holy Spirit*, may not only so do, and pray for the *Spirit*, but also receive the same, and give up to the Dictates and Conduct of it: Which is the *hearty* Desire and *fervent* Prayer of him, that truly wisheth the Welfare and Salvation of all People: And that the *Queen*, and her *Parliament*, with all her *Subjects*, may always be found in that which will tend to Her and Their both *Temporal* and *Eternal Happiness*.

London, *The 10th of the 12th Month*, 1702.   *John Feild.*

E R R A T A.
Title-Page, for *to revenge Wrath*, read a *Revenger to execute Wrath*. P. 6. l. 13. r. *Blessings*.

F I N I S.

A

LETTER

From several Members of the Society for

Reformation of Manners.

To the Most Reverend Father in God

THOMAS

By Divine Providence,

LORD ARCH-BISHOP of *CANTERBURY*.

May it Please Your Grace,

THE several Prosecutions we have made against the Immorality and Prophaneness of the Stage, are a sufficient Proof of our Zeal for the Execution of Her Majesty's Declarations against Immorality and Prophaneness. If we have of late been less Active in this Particular, it is because we found that Her Majesty had by publick Notice given Special Orders to the *Master of the Revels* to take care of those Irregularities. But since the Building of the Playhouse in the *Hay-Market*, it is grown a general Discourse, that the Management of the Company design'd for it, is to be in Mr. *Vanbrook*; the known Character of which Gentleman has very much alarm'd us, and a full consideration of which, has given us so warm a Concern for Her Majesty's Honour, as to inform Your Grace, whose Post and Degree in the Church and State give You so happy an Opportunity of giving Her Majesty an Account of these Reports. Tho' this be given out by both him and his Friends, yet we must suspect the Truth, because 'tis impossible that Her Majesty, who has Declared against Immorality and Prophaneness, and against those Crimes on the Stage, should Act so directly contrary to the End She proposed, as to commit the Management of a Stage to that very Man, who Debauch'd it to a degree beyond the Loosness of all former Times. Both the present Houses were Indicted, and found Guilty by the Court of *Queen's-Bench*, for the several obscene and prophane Expressions in the *Relapse, Provok'd Wife, False Friend*, and the rest of his Plays, in which he is not satisfied to reflect on the Teachers of the Christian Religion, but carries his Impious Fury as far as the *Church, Morality*, and *Religion* it self. Tho' there be not one of his Comedies (as he calls them) but is more remarkable for Irreligion than for Wit and Humour, yet the *Provok'd Wife* is his Master-piece in both, which

made

made the Good and Pious Bishop of *Gloucester*, recommend the Author to Punishment in the House of *Lords*; and he had certainly then been Stigmatiz'd, at least, by a publick Censure of that August Assembly, had he not had the good Fortune to have a Friend that by an admirable Dexterity Warded the Blow, and Diverted the Storm from him which he so justly deserv'd. If then the good Bishop of *Gloucester* with a Pious Zeal attack'd him for what was past, (and we hope almost forgot) how much more must we expect from Your *Grace*'s great and known Piety and Zeal, which will prompt you to inform Her Majesty of what is carrying on without her Knowledge, so much to the Detriment of *Religion* and *Morality*. It was not the Bishop of *Gloucester* alone who was fired with Indignation against this Play of the *Provok'd Wife*, but the Judges themselves having had it Play'd at the *Temple*, were so shock'd at it, that they obliged the Players to leave off in the Middle, and resolv'd never to have a Play Acted there again.

Is then this Author a Man fit for the Government of a Playhouse, whose Writings are in equal Abhorrence to the *Church* and the *State*? Shall he whom the Judges have Condemn'd to that degree, as to renounce the Diversion for the Filth of his Play, be set at the Head, and Management of a Company. But that Your *Grace* may not think this Accusation without Proof, we shall, instead of referring Your *Grace* to the Records in the Court of *Queen's-Bench*, give some few Particulars, for to Transcribe the whole, wou'd be to Transcribe most of what he has Writ.

In his Play call'd, The Provok'd Wife.

‘ But more than all that, you must know, I was afraid of being Damn'd in
‘ those Days, for I kept sneaking cowardly Company, Fellows that went to
‘ Church, and said Grace to their Meat, and had not the least Tincture of Qua-
‘ lity about 'em.

‘ Damn 'em both with all my Heart, and every thing else that daggles a
‘ Pettycoat ; except four generous Whores, with *Betty Sands* at the Head of 'em,
‘ who were Drunk with my Lord *Rake* and I, ten times in a Fortnight.

‘ Sure, if Woman had been ready Created, the Devil instead of being kick'd
‘ down into Hell had been Married.

‘ Pox of my Family.

‘ Pox of her Vertue.

‘ He has Married me, and be damn'd to him.

‘ Pox of the Parson.

‘ Damn Morality, and damn the Watch.

‘ Let me speak and be damn'd.   ⎰ *This is spoken by one in a*

‘ And you and your Wife may be damn'd.   ⎱ *Minister's Habit.*

‘ Stand off and be damn'd.

‘ Damn me, if you han't.

‘ Lord ! What Notions have we silly Women from these old Philosophers of
‘ Vertue, for Vertue is this, and Vertue is that, and Vertue has its own Re-
‘ ward ; Vertue, Vertue is an Ass, and a Gallant is worth Forty on't.

‘ If I should play the Wife and Cuckold him.

‘ That wou'd be playing the downright Wife indeed.

‘ I know according to the strict Statute Law of Religion, I shou'd do
‘ Wrong; but if there were a Court of Chancery in Heaven, I'm sure I shou'd
‘ cast him.

‘ If there were a House of Lords you might.

‘ If you should see your Mistress at a Coronation, dragging her Peacock's
‘ Train, with all her State and Insolence about her, it would strike you with
‘ all the awful Thoughts that Heaven it self could pretend to, from you.

‘ Madam,

' Madam, to oblige your Ladyſhip, he ſhall ſpeak Blaſphemy.

' In hopes thou'lt give me up thy Body, I reſign thee up my Soul.

' A Villain, but a repenting Villain, Stuff which Saints in all Ages have been made of.

' Satan and his Equipage; Woman tempted me, Luſt weakn'd me, and ſo ' the Devil overcame me; as fell *Adam*, ſo fell I.

In his Play call'd, The Relapſe.

' You can't take the Oaths, you're a *Jacobite.*

' Thou may'ſt as well ſay, I can't take Orders becauſe I'm an Atheiſt.

' But pray my Lord how do you diſpoſe of your ſelf on *Sundays* ?

' Why faith Madam——— *Sunday* is a vile Day I muſt confeſs. I intend to ' move for Leave to bring in a Bill, that the Players may work upon it as well ' as the Hackney-Coaches. Tho' this I muſt ſay for the Government, it ' leaves us the Churches to Entertain us, but then again, they begin ſo a- ' bominably Early, a Man muſt riſe by Candle-light to get dreſs'd by the Pſalm.

' Pray which Church does your Lordſhip moſt oblige with your Preſence ?

' Oh St. *James's,* Madam,——— there's much the beſt Company.

' Is there good Preaching too?

' Why faith Madam——I can't tell. A Man muſt have very little to do there ' that can give an account of the Sermon.

' You can give an Account of the Ladies?

' Or I deſerve to be Excommunicated.

' Alas my Lord, I'm the worſt Company in the World at Church, I am apt ' to mind the Prayers, or the Sermon, or——

' One is ſtrangely apt at Church to mind what one ſhould not do.

' Dear *Coupler,* what's to be done.

' Nothing's to be done till the Bride and Bridegroom come to Town.

' Bride and Bridegroom ? Death and Fury, I can't bear that thou ſhould'ſt ' call 'em ſo.

' Why what ſhall I call them, Dog and Cat ?

' Not for the World, that ſounds more like Man and Wife than the t'other.

' Well, if you'll hear of them in no Language, we'll leave them for the Nurſe ' and Chaplain——

' The Devil and the Witch.

' We muſt find what ſtuff they are made of, whether the Churchman be ' chiefly compoſed of the Fleſh or the Spirit, I preſume the former. For as ' Chaplains go, 'tis probable he eats three Pound of Beef to the reading of one ' Chapter, this gives him Carnal Deſires. He wants Money, Preferment, Wine, ' a Whore, therefore we muſt invite him to Supper, give him fat Capons, Sack ' and Sugar, a Purſe of Gold, and a plump Siſter.

' But his Worſhip overflows with his Bounty ; he is not only pleaſed to for- ' give us our Sins, but deſigns thou ſhalt ſquat thy ſelf down in a fat Gooſe ' living.

' Your Worſhip's Goodneſs is unſpeakable ; yet there is one thing ſeems a ' Point of Conſcience, and Conſcience is a tender Babe. If I ſhould bind my ' ſelf for the ſake of this Living to Marry Nurſe, I doubt it may be look'd on ' as a kind of Symony.

' If it were Sacriledge the Living is worth it.

In his Comedy call'd, The Falſe Friend, 1702.

' Pox take ye. ——— The Devil fetch me, *&c.*

' Heaven's Bleſſing muſt needs fall upon ſo dutiful a Son ; but I don't know ' how its Judgments may deal with ſo Indifferent a Lover.

Say

' Say that 'tis true, you are Married to another, and that a ——— ?T'wou'd be
' a Sin to think of any Body but your Husband, and that ——— You are of a
' timorous Nature, and afraid of being Damn'd.

' How have I Lov'd, to Heaven I appeal ; but Heaven does now permit that
' Love no more.

' Why does it then permit us Life and Thought ? Are we deceiv'd in its
' Omnipotence ? Is it reduc'd to find its Pleasure in its Creature's Pain ?

' *Leonora's* Charms turn Vice to Vertue, Treason into Truth ; Nature, who
' has made her the Supream Object of our Desires must needs have design'd
' her the Regulator of our Morals.

' There he goes I'faith ; he seem'd as if he had a Qualm just now ; but he ne-
' ver goes without a dram of Conscience-water about him to set Matters right
' again.

' Speak, or by all the Flame and Fire of Hell Eternal ; speak, or thou art dead.

The most abominable Obscene Expressions which so frequently occur in his
Plays (as if the principal Design of them was to gratifie the lewd and vicious
part of the Audience,and to corrupt the virtuously disposed)are in this black Collection wholly omitted. We are asham'd to disgust Your *Grace's* Eyes with
such Stuff that is not fit to Read. What then can recommend this Gentleman
to such a Post ? No Religion, and much Assurance ? But my Lord, Your *Grace*
is too great an Example of Piety and Justice, to suffer Her Majesty to be longer
Ignorant of a Design so very Prejudicial to *Christianity*, and the *Morality* of the
whole Nation ; which if she knew, her Virtue and Piety wonld put a stop to
our Fears and Apprehensions.

We have discharged our Duty in putting it into Your *Grace's* Hands to prevent so great a Mischief to *Religion*. And we are entirely satisfied that by it we
may be secure of having Her Majesty acquainted with it, and by consequence
these difficulties remov'd, by removing the Cause.

London, *December* 10th. 1704.

F I N I S.